The Unofficial TikTok Cookbook

The Unofficial TikTok Cookbook

75 Internet-Breaking Recipes for Snacks, Drinks, Treats, and More!

Valentina Mussi @sweetportfolio

ADAMS MEDIA

NEW YORK   LONDON   TORONTO   SYDNEY   NEW DELHI

Adams Media
An Imprint of Simon & Schuster, Inc.
100 Technology Center Drive
Stoughton, Massachusetts 02072

First Adams Media hardcover edition June 2021

ADAMS MEDIA and colophon are trademarks of Simon & Schuster.

For information about special discounts for bulk purchases, please contact Simon & Schuster Special Sales at 1-866-506-1949 or business@simonandschuster.com.

The Simon & Schuster Speakers Bureau can bring authors to your live event. For more information or to book an event contact the Simon & Schuster Speakers Bureau at 1-866-248-3049 or visit our website at www.simonspeakers.com.

Interior design by Erin Alexander
Illustrations by Priscilla Yuen
Photographs by Harper Point Photography

Manufactured in the United States of America

4 2022

Library of Congress Cataloging-in-Publication Data
Names: Mussi, Valentina, author.
Title: The unofficial TikTok cookbook / Valentina Mussi @sweetportfolio.
Description: Stoughton, MA: Adams Media, an imprint of Simon & Schuster, Inc., 2021 | Series: Unofficial cookbook | Includes index.
Identifiers: LCCN 2021000303 | ISBN 9781507215852 (hc) | ISBN 9781507215869 (ebook)
Subjects: LCSH: Snack foods. | TikTok. | Web-based instruction. | LCGFT: Cookbooks.
Classification: LCC TX740 .M87 2021 | DDC 641.5/3--dc23
LC record available at https://lccn.loc.gov/2021000303

ISBN 978-1-5072-1585-2
ISBN 978-1-5072-1586-9 (ebook)

To my Abuelo Rodrigo;
my parents, Monica and Marcello;
my siblings, Stefano and Dominique;
and my cat, Alphonso Mango.

Contents

CHAPTER 1 Viral Recipes, Explained · 15

CHAPTER 2

Fun Drinks · 27

Breakfast Hacks · 51

Quick and Easy Snacks · 77

CHAPTER 5

Lunch and Dinner · 105

CHAPTER 6

Desserts, Desserts, and More Desserts · 129

Introduction

Everyone's seen a regular cheeseburger, but what about a burger topped with fried mozzarella? 🔥 TBH, who wants the same old ice cream cone when you can indulge in scoops of edible cookie dough loaded with sprinkles? And why go for a boring slice of pizza when there's pizza mac 'n' cheese?! The ability to share photos and videos of what we eat, when we eat it, has made us high-key obsessed with food. Viral TikTok videos, kitchen YouTube channels, and chef Instagram accounts show off amazing dishes you can practically taste through your phone. And the more interesting, colorful, and over-the-top, the better!

This is the ✨ new food culture ✨: the ultimate glow-up from fancy fine dining we pretend we have the cash for and traditional meals our parents made us. It's time for post-worthy dishes that will impress your followers and have your friends texting you for the recipe! *The Unofficial TikTok Cookbook* embraces microwaves, air fryers, and waffle makers for seventy-five of the most eye-grabbing, easy-to-make treats you can't share fast enough.

You'll find popular creations like Pancake Cereal, Dalgona Coffee Latte, and Cookie Mug Cake, plus some never-before-seen recipes to help you go viral. Organized by chapter based on the type of dish, this cookbook has something for every mood and situation. Most of the recipes have supershort prep times, and all can be made without complex techniques, fancy kitchens, or weird, pricey ingredients. You'll also discover social media insights and tips to help you take great photos and videos of your master-pieces and share them effectively so they reach more viewers.

Whether you dream of becoming a social media influencer, you're a passionate food lover, or you just want something new and delicious to share with your friends, this book is full of insider food tricks to help you along the way! Use the Notes pages at the back of the book to keep track of how your creations and videos turn out, or to brainstorm your own viral recipes. 🥰

Viral Recipes, Explained

It happens first on TikTok! All the newest trends, memes, and viral challenges are here—way before they spread into the other corners of the Internet like Facebook or Instagram. TikTok is *the* trendsetter for Internet culture, and that includes food recipes. From whipped coffee to pancake cereal, you got to see it happen on TikTok first.

This chapter will give you the basics and insider details for everything TikTok. I'll go through all the key app features and top trends and answer juicy questions like how I got my account verified (and how you can too), what my must-have kitchen equipment is for making viral recipe videos, and which editing apps are my absolute faves. It's the cooking guide made exclusively #foryou. 🥰

A (Very) Brief History

TikTok might have started as a music-based lip-synching and dancing app, but it quickly turned into a social network with everything from funny stories and supercute animal videos to the tips, facts, and advice on #edutok. Its advanced algorithms determine #foryou which content you'll like the most!

And one of the best things to come from the app is the food hacks. While our parents and grandparents learned to cook from passed down family recipes, cutting them out of newspapers and magazines, and watching chefs on TV, learning how to cook nowadays is a *lot* different thanks to #TikTokFood. We're now finding recipes mostly as 1-minute videos. The videos are super-fast-paced, straight to the point, and focused on whatever's trending ATM.

Modern home cooks are whipping up the most unique, delicious, and aesthetic dishes and teaching others how to make them. They're building communities (#welovepizza is a whole mood) and strong bonds with their followers. When someone in their audience has a question about a dish, cooking time, or technique—or just wants to give a compliment or feedback—they can send a private message to the user or post a comment on the video.

#Trending

One of the best things about TikTok is the trends. Every time you open the app, there's a new trend, exciting challenge, or popular sound. Probably the most notable TikTok food trend is the dalgona coffee, or whipped coffee. Did you ever imagine you could turn something as basic as instant coffee into a beautiful fluffy cream?? I definitely didn't.

This actually led me to create my own TikTok trend: whipped milk. After dalgona coffee became popular, I knew I had to come up with a noncaffeinated version. A lot of TikTok users don't like the taste of strong coffee—not to mention, I can only handle about one cup a day myself. I needed to preserve the fluffy qualities of dalgona and make it into a coffee-free alternative. I combined heavy whipping cream with different flavored powders and syrups and made Whipped Cocoa, Whipped Strawberry Milk, Whipped Matcha Latte, and more than twenty other creations that went viral. (You'll find a few of my faves in Chapter 2.)

The next big trend was pancake cereal and other cereal foods. It's the cutest trend ever because, seriously, anything made into a mini version of itself is adorable. It's more tedious to make, sure, but sooo fun, so creators were immediately making mini cereal versions of everything—croissant cereal, cookie cereal, pizza cereal, and more!

#Foodfam

One of the coolest parts of the TikTok food recipe explosion is that it's created a global kitchen. Because anyone with a smartphone can make a dish and post it online, people from around the world are sharing their favorite foods and introducing viewers to things they may not have seen or even heard of otherwise.

And anyone can come up with a cool food concept and start a trend! Most "famous" online chefs have never received any formal training. Instead, they're food lovers who have fun experimenting in the kitchen. Their charm comes from the fact that they create recipes that can be replicated by almost anyone, using basic ingredients and tools most already have at home.

It's a Look

There are four leading social media platforms to watch food videos on: YouTube, Facebook, Instagram, and, of course, TikTok.

The two more "old-school" ones are YouTube and Facebook, where videos can be over an hour long, although the average length for a YouTube video is 11 minutes, and a little less than 7 minutes for a Facebook video. These recipe videos tend to be geared toward older generations and are similar to the traditional cooking TV shows our parents loved. For the most part, there is a host in charge of speaking to the audience, and there is a bit of chatter during the video (an introduction, a couple of jokes, and some commentary). Both of these platforms allow for engaging elements (e.g., likes and comments). Facebook also allows for shares and livestreaming.

But we want things to be shorter and more to the point. (Who's got time for a 10-minute monologue on why you love making bread?? Just show me how to make it already!) That's why platforms like Instagram and TikTok have become more popular. Both allow users to like, comment, and share videos too, but videos are just 1 minute long to cut out all the boring stuff. Plus, both platforms have a livestreaming feature.

The key differences between TikTok and Instagram are that TikTok lets you duet and stitch videos, meaning you can take another creator's video and film your reaction to it or even add a clip of it into your own video. TikTok also allows users to add music to their videos or take another person's video sound and reuse it in their own.

A good TikTok recipe tells the whole story fast and combines multiple scenes. The transitions are smooth, there is audio (either a song, sound, or voice-over), and there is a beginning and an end. (That means you should start your recipe by showing your ingredients and end with the final product.) Your viewers need to be able to understand what you are making and how, just from watching the 1-minute video.

Keeping It Simple

Knowing how TikTok stands out from the other platforms helps you decide what is a good fit for a recipe video. TikTok recipes are characterized by their simple ingredients (a lot of instant batters and premade doughs) that can be found at any grocery store, and by the appliances used. Microwaves, air fryers, and waffle makers are your best friend when cooking for TikTok. Luckily, nearly everyone has these, whether in their kitchen, office, or even dorm room. The goal is to teach your audience how to simplify their cooking and still create a dish that is #EXTRA! ✨

In addition to step-by-step instructions, what really makes a TikTok recipe are the beauty shots. The cheese pulls, the pouring of chocolate syrup, the steam coming off a hot plate of pasta, the swirl of whipped cream, and the lifting of a spoonful of dessert—these are the shots that get you excited and make simple dishes go from just food to #foodporn. Focus on the aesthetic dishes and indulgent treats (what are calories...?); TikTok recipes are all about the fun!

What You'll Need

To become the next big TikTok chef, you'll need some things. From basic ingredients to editing apps, here's everything that will help make your recipes—and videos—a success.

Ingredients

TikTok recipes are simple and require just a few ingredients that you can easily find at the grocery store. Stock up on these must-haves:

- Heavy whipping cream for whipped milk
- String cheese for air fryer mozzarella sticks, pizza rolls, and more
- Complete ("just add water") pancake mix for all kinds of mini pancakes and fried cookies
- Crescent rolls for pizza rolls and cookie butter croissants
- Chocolate chip cookie dough because nobody has the time to make things from scratch

You'll also need the basics that are in pretty much every baked good: granulated sugar, all-purpose flour, eggs, baking powder, unsalted butter, milk, and nonstick cooking spray.

Appliances

The point of TikTok recipes is to create extravagant dishes the easiest way possible—and with little cleanup. Here are the staple cooking appliances you will use in the recipes in this book:

1. **Air fryer.** I am *not* exaggerating when I say that I live for this thing. It makes cooking, baking, and frying *sooo* easy. There's no need for fatty oil, and it cuts the cooking time in half. Get one with at least a 3.5-quart basket.
2. **Waffle maker.** I use it to make more than just plain old waffles; you'll see just how flexible this appliance can be.

3. **Electric mixer.** All cooks need a mixer! They are the key to all the whipped TikTok trends. Making dalgona coffee and whipped milk without it would require some serious hand-whisking action.

If you don't have one of these already, you know what to put on your wish list! You can also borrow a friend's or family member's in a pinch.

Filming Equipment

When making TikToks, there's no need for fancy DSLR cameras. I film all my video content straight from my phone! Here is a rundown of my filming setup:

Cameras

All my videos are filmed with an iPhone 12 Pro Max camera. I film at a 9:16 ratio format (vertical) and set my phone camera settings to record at 1080p HD for a high-quality video.

Lighting

When it comes to lighting, I try to film close to a natural light source like the window in my kitchen because it's convenient and it gives food videos a really nice tone. Of course, when it's cloudy out or when I'm filming at night, my kitchen is not so bright and I have to use artificial light. In these cases, I recommend the following:

1. **A small ring light.** These are sold online and at electronics stores. They're a cheap option and can light up your subject really well.
2. **A softbox lighting kit.** This is a slightly more expensive option. Kits usually start at around $50 and go up to $200. They're great for when you film a lot of content at home but don't have a consistent source of natural light, and when you want to light up a bigger room.

Tripods

I use two types of tripods for all of my cooking videos, depending on the angles I'm trying to get:

1. **Overhead tripod mount.** This isn't actually a tripod but more of an arm that clamps to any table or counter for overhead videos. I use this angle especially when baking because I tend to add a lot of different ingredients into the bowl, and I like the bird's-eye view of each ingredient being added.

2. **Traditional tripod with phone adapter.** I use this when recording videos of myself and for straight-on and low angles of food—for example, when I make a supercheesy dish, and I want to lift it for the cheese-pull effect.

Editing Apps

The TikTok app has great in-app features to edit your videos, but sometimes you want to use outside music, fix the lighting, or add text with different fonts.

My favorite app is Kinemaster. It works like an advanced computer video editing app, but straight from your phone! You can put together clips, add music, and edit specific elements like saturation, vibrancy, and temperature. For even more editing options, check out InShot, Zoomerang, and Voloco. These let you add filters, transition effect, and voice-changing features that work superwell for voice-over videos.

Beating the Algorithm

No one knows exactly how the TikTok algorithm works—and HQ doesn't exactly disclose it. Why? Well, they don't fully understand it either! The algorithm has a mind of its own based on the information the TikTok engineers feed it.

Before I can tell you what's helped me "beat" the algorithm, I need to get a *little* technical and explain what exactly an algorithm is in the social media world. An algorithm's job is to comb through content and determine which videos you would be most interested in seeing based on the info the app has gathered about you (age, location, interests, likes, dislikes). What you know as the For You page (FYP) is the TikTok home screen where you scroll through videos from all different users. The TikTok algorithm shows you videos it thinks you'd enjoy, and it records which you interacted with (liked, commented, shared, or followed), watched all of, replayed, or simply scrolled past. The algorithm learns from all of your interactions to continue to feed you content that you are likely to enjoy.

Taking the algorithm into account, you should optimize your content in order to get more views. Here are my top tips to land on more people's For You page:

1. **Catch their attention early.** TikTok is a platform where videos are played automatically, and with just a quick swipe up, your video is gone forever from your audience's phone. You want to stop them from scrolling by catching their attention immediately, so the first couple of seconds are critical. The best way to do this when it comes to a food video is by showing a preview of the final product or by announcing what the video is about. A text bubble or voice-over saying something like "Today I'm teaching you how to make Pizza in a Mug" is a great way of getting people to stop scrolling and watch your video.

2. **Length matters!** TikTok lets users upload videos up to 1 minute long, but most of us aren't down to watch anything longer than 30 seconds. Don't get me wrong, I'd *love* to be able to include every single shot of food I film, but most people don't have the patience to watch a full minute before swiping. You are trying to engage your audience and keep them entertained, so less is more! (Sometimes I do post videos longer than 30 seconds, but only when I'm confident that my recipe and storytelling are so engaging that my viewer will want to watch the whole thing. 😋)

3. **Teach 'em something.** People need a reason to follow you. I've been able to grow my account to over one million followers because I teach viewers how to make food. Keep this in mind when creating your own content! Don't just share a mac 'n' cheese video—teach the viewer how to make it! Share tips and twists for how they can re-create it themselves. When someone finds your video on the FYP and realizes you give good advice, they'll be more likely to follow you.

Getting That Clout

Growing your TikTok is about more than just beating the algorithm and landing on the FYP. It's about showing people who you are and giving them a reason to follow you. Growing your following can only happen when you foster a community, treat your audience with respect, and be kind despite the trolls.

Here are some things to keep in mind when you begin to establish yourself as a TikTok content creator:

1. **Reply to comments.** People love it when a creator replies to or likes their comment. It builds a relationship and makes them want to follow you. But as your account grows and your videos go viral, this will become more difficult, since there will be more comments to keep up with. Try to designate a couple of minutes every day to answering people's questions and thanking them when they give you a compliment.

2. **Build up a thick skin.** When you post something, you're giving anyone online the right to comment...and not everyone is nice when it comes to sharing their thoughts. I get countless mean comments on my content, and the moment your video goes viral, you probably will too. You need to learn to focus on the positive comments (because there's usually a ton of them! 🥰) and ignore the haters.

3. **Follow trends.** Online trends tend to be really short-lived, so jump on them as soon as you can. Being an early adopter is a great way to go viral! If you see that a sound is starting to trend, film your video and post it ASAP. Part of the TikTok experience is looking at the top videos on the discover page, and that's how you get the hype.

4. **Don't be afraid to experiment.** Being a trendsetter is just as important as adopting trends early on. You'll get a ton of traction and inspire other users to follow suit. I've accomplished this by making cookie mug cakes, whipped milk, and air fryer snacks; experimenting helped me establish myself as a recipe developer and full-time online content creator.

A lot of people also associate getting verified with clout. 👁️👄👁️ But getting verified on TikTok is mostly a vanity metric. Take it from me: There's no advantage to being verified other than users knowing that your account/brand is legit. The TikTok app looks the same for verified creators, and we don't get any unique features.

If you *do* want to be verified, there's no way to request verification on TikTok. Instead, the app decides when and who to grant it to. In my case, I was verified about three months after creating my account when I had close to one hundred thousand followers. I didn't see any changes in my account or engagement rate.

Boosting Your Platform

Once you've gained a following, there are three main ways of monetizing your TikTok platform:

1. **Join the TikTok Creator Program.** In fall 2020, TikTok launched the TikTok Creator Program, which provides revenue to its app creators. To be eligible to join, creators must have ten thousand or more followers, be at least eighteen years old, and live in the US.
2. **Go Live.** Going live is a great way to build a deeper connection with your following! When creators go live, they host a livestream and start to record themselves while other users are notified and join their live video. Creators can talk directly to their followers; they can ask questions and post visible comments to all viewers. During livestreaming sessions, followers can also send tokens to the creator, which are a kind of online payment.
3. **Partner with Brands and Post Ads.** This is the top source of income for most online content creators. Companies hire influencers to film videos that introduce their followers to their product and share their message.

One other note about brands: If there is a brand that you particularly enjoy, post about them and tag them! This is how you get their attention. Over 90 percent of my content is organic and unpaid; when you see me cooking and using the same brands over and over, it's a genuine recommendation. (Posting organically about these brands has led me to sign deals!)

Adding Your Own Twist

Now that you've learned the insider details of becoming a #TikTokChef, it's time to start experimenting (and filming) for yourself! Cooking and filming at the same time can be tricky at first, but with a little practice you'll be a pro. Use this book as a jumping-off point for your own unique creations. Interested in trying whipped milk, but not a fan of strawberries? Switch out the strawberry powder for a different flavor. Love the idea of the Fried Mozzarella Burger but don't eat meat? Swap it for a veggie burger patty to make it your own! Want to "pizza-fy" your Garlic Turtle Bread? Add in pepperoni, marinara, and mozzarella, and you've got something totally new. There are virtually no rules here: Just have fun and cook what you're craving the most. 😋

CHAPTER 2

Fun Drinks

Dalgona Coffee Latte

This is the recipe that broke the whole Internet. It's arguably the most significant coffee drink since the Pumpkin Spice Latte. The best part? It's made with ingredients you probably already have.

SERVES 1

3 tablespoons instant coffee
3 tablespoons hot water
3 tablespoons granulated sugar
¾ cup whole milk

1. In a medium bowl, combine coffee, water, and sugar. Using an electric mixer set to high speed or a whisk, beat 10 minutes until stiff peaks form.

2. Fill an 8-ounce glass ¾ full of ice and then add milk. Spoon coffee mixture on top.

Kitchen Hacks

Getting the coffee mixture to fluff up can feel like a long process, especially when whisking it by hand! If you don't have an electric mixer, no worries: Just use a shaker bottle (the ones with a round metal ball) instead. Pour coffee, water, and sugar into the bottle, and shake up for a couple of minutes.

Whipped Strawberry Milk

Here's a supereasy three-ingredient take on the drink you've loved since forever. It has a fluffy, sweet topping poured over iced milk that is bound to get you a ton of views. Snap your pics quickly before the whipped milk melts! For a ✦ vegan version ✦ use coconut whipping cream instead of heavy whipping cream and almond or oat milk instead of whole milk. Chill the coconut whipping cream overnight to get the perfect fluffy texture.

SERVES 1

2 tablespoons strawberry-flavored powder
½ cup heavy whipping cream
¾ cup whole milk

1. In a medium bowl, add strawberry powder and cream. Using an electric mixer set to medium-high speed or a whisk, beat 3 minutes until soft peaks form.

2. Fill an 8-ounce glass ¾ full of ice and then pour in milk.

3. Spoon strawberry whipped mixture on top of milk. Quick: Snap a pic and drink it before the whipped milk melts!

#ForYou Tips

To make your whipped milk creations come to life for the camera, use taffy candies or fondant and a Sharpie Permanent Marker. You can use the marker to draw eyes or a face on the outside of the glass (it comes off with rubbing alcohol! 👁️👄👁️). To make your strawberry milk look like a pig, cut a square pink taffy candy in half diagonally and place the triangles on top of your drink to make ears. For a unicorn, form a 3½" cylinder of fondant into a teardrop shape and then twist it into a horn and stick it in the top of the drink.

Matcha Milkshake

Achieving the perfect milk-to-ice-cream ratio in a milkshake is no easy task, but I've got ya, boo. Here is how to make the perfect caffeinated, thick milkshake to satisfy your sugar and energy cravings.

SERVES 1

5 (½-cup) scoops vanilla ice cream

2¼ teaspoons matcha powder, divided

¼ cup whole milk

Canned whipped cream

1. In a blender, combine ice cream, 2 teaspoons matcha powder, and milk at the highest speed for 1 minute.

2. Pour into a tall glass and top with a big swirl of whipped cream. Lightly sprinkle remaining ¼ teaspoon matcha powder on top.

Golden Milk Latte

Golden milk is a traditional Indian drink with tons of potential health benefits and a deep yellow color that have made it superpopular on social media. A turmeric drink might sound a little unconventional, but trust me, it tastes *amazing*.

SERVES 1

2 tablespoons ground turmeric

⅛ teaspoon ground ginger

¼ teaspoon ground cinnamon

1 tablespoon honey

1 cup whole milk

1. In a small saucepan over medium-high heat, combine all ingredients. Cook 4 minutes, whisking continuously while cooking.

2. Pour into a large mug and drink immediately.

White Hot Chocolate

You've probably spent your whole life drinking hot cocoa, but what about White Hot Chocolate? This will be your new favorite for staying warm and cozy all winter. 😊

SERVES 1

1 cup whole milk
¼ cup white chocolate chips
½ teaspoon vanilla extract
¼ cup mini marshmallows

1. In a small saucepan over medium-low heat, combine milk, chocolate chips, and vanilla. Cook while whisking 5 minutes until chocolate is melted.

2. Serve in a tall mug topped with marshmallows.

Whipped Matcha Latte

Matcha lattes are the perfect drink to satisfy your caffeine cravings! Matcha is known for its intense tea flavor and potential health benefits, like antioxidants. It's time to give your basic matcha latte the ultimate glow-up.

SERVES 1

1½ teaspoons matcha powder

⅓ cup heavy whipping cream

1½ tablespoons granulated sugar

¾ cup whole milk

1. In a medium bowl, combine matcha powder, cream, and sugar. Using an electric mixer set to medium-high speed or a whisk, beat 3 minutes until soft peaks form.

2. Heat milk either with a milk-heating frother or in a small saucepan over medium-high heat 4 minutes until milk begins to steam.

3. Pour milk into a tall mug and spoon whipped matcha mixture on top.

Kitchen Hacks

The matcha used to make drinks is known as ceremonial matcha. It's the highest-quality matcha; it has a deeper, more vibrant green color and a slightly stronger taste than culinary-grade matcha. This is the kind used in traditional Japanese tea ceremonies, but it can be a bit hard to find. Culinary-grade matcha is a great option if you don't have ceremonial matcha on hand; it's sold at most grocery stores and is more affordable. 😋

Whipped Piña Colada

Fruity beverages don't always have to come in smoothie form. This is a fun, alcohol-free version of everybody's favorite tropical drink. No need to pack your bags; this recipe brings the Caribbean right to you!

SERVES 1

3 tablespoons canned pineapple juice

⅓ cup heavy whipping cream

1 cup ice cubes

2 tablespoons canned coconut cream

1 cup unsweetened coconut milk

2 tablespoons granulated sugar

1. In a medium bowl, combine juice and whipping cream. Using an electric mixer set to medium-high speed or a whisk, beat 5 minutes until soft peaks form.

2. In a blender, combine ice, coconut cream, coconut milk, and sugar at the highest speed for 1 minute.

3. Pour blended mixture in a tall glass or 12-ounce Mason jar. Top glass with whipped pineapple mixture and drink with a straw.

Whipped Cocoa

Chocolate milk is *the* classic drink we all remember from childhood. Some say classics shouldn't change, but I say why not make them even better?! Here's how to make chocolate milk more exciting and still bring back the nostalgia.

SERVES 1

1 teaspoon cocoa powder
2 tablespoons granulated sugar
⅓ cup heavy whipping cream
¾ cup whole milk

1. In a medium bowl, combine cocoa, sugar, and cream. Using an electric mixer set to medium-high speed or a whisk, beat 3 minutes until medium peaks form.

2. Fill an 8-ounce glass ¾ full of ice and then pour in milk.

3. Spoon whipped cocoa mixture on top of milk. Drink with a straw.

Kitchen Hacks

Use this recipe as the base to make all kinds of flavored whipped milk! I've made whipped cookie butter, whipped hazelnut spread, whipped key lime—even whipped soy sauce. As long as you've got heavy whipping cream, anything can happen. 🐨

Orange Cream Float

Floats are drinks from the 1950s made with ice cream and soda. Let's give this delicious treat the comeback it deserves! Channel your inner hipster, add a vintage filter, and sip away.

SERVES 1

2 (½-cup) scoops vanilla ice cream, divided

1 (12-ounce) can orange soda

Canned whipped cream

1. Place 1 scoop ice cream in a tall glass. Fill glass ¾ full with soda.

2. Carefully add second scoop of ice cream and top with a big swirl of whipped cream.

Brown Sugar Boba Milk Tea

This drink from Taiwan has quickly taken over social media. It's named after boba tea, but actually isn't made with any tea—just milk. *Boba* is what the round tapioca pearls at the bottom of the drink are called. There are tons of different types of boba, but the most popular is black tapioca. You can stick with the classic fave or try out other boba like the mini or clear versions.

SERVES 2

4¼ cups water, divided
½ cup tapioca pearls
¼ cup dark brown sugar
2 cups whole milk

1. In a medium saucepan over medium-high heat, bring 4 cups water to a boil and add tapioca pearls. Simmer 6 minutes over medium heat, strain, and add to a large bowl filled with ice water for 1 minute, then strain again. Return to saucepan.

2. Over medium-high heat, combine cooked tapioca pearls with remaining water and sugar using a wooden spoon. Cook 14 minutes or until sugar thickens and becomes a syrup.

3. Add 4 tablespoons boba mixture to an 8-ounce glass, carefully swirling around to cover the sides of the glass. Pour milk on top. Repeat in a second glass with remaining ingredients.

Kitchen Hacks

Use a thick boba straw, either plastic or metal, to mix the milk with the boba pearls and syrup. The straw's sharp end should be facing down; use it to sip the drink and chew the pearls.

Pumpkin Spice Frappé

Pumpkin spice is the OG trendy social media drink. I say we make it a year-round thing instead of having to wait for fall. And don't worry—making your own pumpkin spice seasoning is supereasy too!

SERVES 1

1 teaspoon ground cinnamon

⅛ teaspoon ground nutmeg

⅛ teaspoon ground ginger

⅛ teaspoon ground cloves

1 shot espresso

1 cup whole milk

1 cup ice cubes

3 tablespoons instant vanilla pudding powder

1. In a small bowl, whisk together all spices.

2. Pour espresso into a blender. Add spice blend, milk, ice, and pudding and blend at the highest speed for 1 minute, until no large ice chunks are left.

3. Serve in a 16-ounce glass.

Lychee Boba Lemonade

Here's another caffeine-free boba drink, this time with the superpopular popping boba, little jelly balls full of sweet fruit juice that burst in your mouth before you even bite into them. They will *for sure* take any drink to the next level!

SERVES 2

1 cup canned lychees with syrup

1 cup lemonade

1 cup water

1 cup ice cubes

8 tablespoons lychee popping boba

1. In a blender, combine lychees, lemonade, water, and ice and blend at the highest speed for 1 minute.

2. Add 4 tablespoons each of popping boba to the bottom of two 16-ounce cups. Fill with lychee mixture. Drink with boba straws.

Kitchen Hacks

Popping boba can be found online, as well as at almost any Asian grocery store. It comes in all sorts of flavors; the most popular ones are lychee, mango, and strawberry. They're mostly added to drinks, but you can experiment with adding them to desserts too! 😋

Dragon Fruit Lemonade Frappé

Move over açaí, dragon fruit (also known as *pitaya*) is the new rage on TikTok. This exotic fruit is a *gorgeous* magenta color and has cute little black seeds. It's the perfect addition to any drink or smoothie bowl.

SERVES 1

¼ cup frozen dragon fruit chunks

¼ cup frozen mango chunks

¾ cup lemonade

¾ cup coconut water

1. In a blender, combine all ingredients. Blend 1 minute at high speed until smooth.

2. Fill a 16-ounce glass ¾ full with ice and pour fruit mixture on top.

Pink Coconut Drink

I bet you've seen tons of photos on social media of a mysterious pink drink. It looks kind of intimidating to make, but this recipe is supereasy. The key is fresh strawberries.

SERVES 1

1 cup sliced fresh strawberries, divided

1 cup vanilla-flavored coconut milk

1 tablespoon hibiscus tea powder

2 tablespoons granulated sugar

1 cup ice cubes

1. In a blender, combine ¾ cup strawberries, coconut milk, tea powder, sugar, and ice. Blend 1 minute at high speed, until there are no large ice chips left.

2. Serve in a tall glass topped with remaining strawberry slices.

#ForYou Tips

Serve your drink in a reusable cup with a lid and a straw. Hold the cup up toward the sky in one hand, making sure the sun is behind you. Snap a pic and edit it on your phone to enhance the pink tint of the drink.

Breakfast Hacks

Mermaid Smoothie Bowl

Goodbye regular old smoothie; hello delicious smoothie bowl! Smoothie bowls are thicker than the classic drink and make the perfect canvas for colorful toppings shaped in fun patterns (try cutting the banana slices into stars). This mermaid-inspired bowl uses an algae powder called *Blue Majik* that's loaded with nutrients and turns the smoothie a bright blue color. Add edible pearls and use a mermaid tail and shell molds to complete the look.

SERVES 1

2 large frozen bananas

2 cups frozen pineapple chunks

½ cup unsweetened coconut milk

2 teaspoons Blue Majik

¼ cup granola

2 tablespoons chia seeds

½ large banana, peeled and sliced

¼ cup chopped fresh strawberries

2 tablespoons honey

1. In a blender, combine frozen bananas, pineapple, coconut milk, and Blue Majik. Blend at high speed 45 seconds, stop and scrape the edges of the cup, and blend another 45 seconds until thick and creamy.

2. Using a soft silicone spatula, scoop smoothie into a small bowl.

3. Flatten the top with the spatula and add granola, chia seeds, sliced banana, and strawberries on top. Drizzle with honey.

#For You Tips

To film a #viral smoothie bowl recipe video, make sure you are near a window or a good light source and film separate clips of each step in this recipe. Also, try to switch the angle as often as you can to keep the video exciting. For example, film the pouring of your smoothie at a straight-on angle and the placement of the toppings at an overhead angle. Edit all of the best clips together, upload, add a funny caption, and don't forget the trending hashtags!

Air Fryer Soufflé Pancakes

This is a quick and easy version of the superviral, superfun Japanese jiggly soufflé pancake. These pancakes are usually cooked on a stovetop and take time and patience, but here is a much less complicated way to make the fluffiest pancakes you'll ever try! Serve them with butter and maple syrup, or jam and fresh berries.

SERVES 4

3 large eggs

1 tablespoon vegetable oil

2 tablespoons whole milk

1 teaspoon vanilla extract

¼ cup all-purpose flour

1 teaspoon granulated sugar

1 teaspoon white vinegar

1. Preheat air fryer to 250°F. Spray four 4″ ramekins with nonstick cooking spray.

2. Separate whites and yolks of 2 eggs into two medium bowls. Add white of third egg to egg white bowl and discard yolk or save for another time.

3. Add oil, milk, and vanilla to bowl with yolks and stir to combine. Slowly sift in flour and mix well.

4. Add sugar and vinegar to bowl with egg whites. Using an electric mixer set to high speed or a whisk, beat 4 minutes until stiff peaks form.

5. Fold egg yolk mixture into egg white mixture. Be careful not to overmix.

6. Transfer batter to a large plastic bag. Snip off one corner of bag, making a 1″ hole.

7. Carefully pipe batter in a swirling pattern into ramekins, leaving 1½″ of space at the top.

8. Place ramekins in air fryer and cook 10 minutes. Serve immediately.

#ForYou Tips

If you decide to share these on social media, make a slo-mo video of you shaking the serving plate. The soufflé pancakes are so airy that they will jiggle!

Pink Protein Smoothie Bowl

It's pink, it's delicious, and it's good for you too! This beautiful smoothie is packed with protein and yields the thickest, creamiest texture *ever*. No watery smoothie bowl #fail for you!

SERVES 1

1 cup frozen dragon fruit chunks

1 cup frozen whole raspberries

1 cup frozen mango chunks

½ cup unsweetened coconut milk

3 tablespoons vanilla protein powder

¼ cup coconut flakes

2 tablespoons flaxseed

¼ cup goji berries

1 large kiwi, peeled and sliced

1. In a blender, combine all frozen fruit, coconut milk, and protein powder. Blend together 2 minutes until ingredients are incorporated and become a thick smoothie paste.

2. Using a soft silicone spatula, scoop smoothie into a small bowl. Flatten the top with spatula.

3. Top with coconut, flaxseed, goji berries, and kiwi.

Cookie Butter Croissants

This recipe takes store-bought croissant dough to a whole new level. It turns it into a delicious breakfast snack boosted by the rich flavor and crunchy texture of popular European speculoos cookies.

SERVES 8

1 (8-ounce) can crescent rolls

4 tablespoons cookie butter spread

4 speculoos cookies, crushed

1. Preheat oven to 375°F. Line a large baking sheet with parchment paper.

2. Unroll crescent roll dough, separate triangles, and place each triangle on prepared baking sheet.

3. Add ½ tablespoon cookie butter to the center of each triangle and top with ⅛ of the crushed cookies. Roll up each dough triangle, starting at the widest part, into a crescent shape.

4. Bake 10 minutes. Serve while still warm.

Instead of cookie butter, use any spread you've got handy! Or take them to the next level by stuffing them with cheese. 😋

Kitchen Hacks

One-Pan Breakfast Sandwich

Here are step-by-step instructions to nail the breakfast #hack you've seen all over TikTok. This is perfect when you've only got one clean pan and you don't want to do any extra dishes (and TBH who wants to do dishes *ever*?).

SERVES 1

2 medium eggs

¼ teaspoon salt

¼ teaspoon ground black pepper

1 tablespoon salted butter

2 slices white bread

2 slices sharp Cheddar cheese

1. Whisk eggs in a medium bowl and add salt and pepper.

2. Use butter to grease a large skillet over medium heat.

3. Pour eggs into skillet and lightly twist pan while holding handle to create an even egg coat.

4. Place bread slices on top of egg mixture and cook 2 minutes.

5. Using a spatula, carefully flip bread to allow egg to finish cooking 1 more minute. Top each slice with Cheddar cheese and let melt.

6. Once egg is fully cooked and cheese is melted, place 1 bread slice on the other to create a sandwich.

Pink Chia Pudding

Oatmeal is so yesterday! This is the perfect meal-prep breakfast for zero effort on mornings when you wish you could've stayed in bed. Just make the pudding the night before and leave it in the fridge overnight.

SERVES 4

2 cups fresh whole raspberries

2 cups unsweetened coconut milk

3 tablespoons maple syrup

½ tablespoon vanilla extract

⅓ cup chia seeds

1. In a food processor or blender, combine raspberries, coconut milk, maple syrup, and vanilla at medium speed for 30 seconds.

2. In a medium bowl, combine raspberry mixture with chia seeds.

3. Divide mixture among four small jars or containers. Cover and refrigerate overnight.

4. Enjoy the next day or store in the fridge for up to 2 days.

Kitchen Hacks

Chia pudding can be made into any flavor using the same base of 2 cups milk mixed with ⅓ cup chia seeds. You can add 2 tablespoons cocoa powder instead of the raspberries to make chocolate pudding or add 2 teaspoons matcha powder for a green tea-flavored pudding.

Chocolate Chip
French Toast Casserole

For when you want to have #brunch without dropping all your money in bottom-less mimosas—or leaving your house. Classic French toast can be a pain to make, but this recipe makes it easy.

SERVES 4

6 large eggs

1 (14-ounce) can evaporated milk

1 (15-ounce) can sweetened condensed milk

1 tablespoon vanilla extract

½ tablespoon ground cinnamon

1 loaf brioche bread, cut into 1½" cubes

1 cup milk chocolate chips

3 tablespoons powdered sugar

½ cup maple syrup

1. Coat a 3-quart casserole dish with nonstick cooking spray.

2. In a large bowl, combine eggs, evaporated milk, condensed milk, vanilla, and cinnamon. Using an electric mixer set to medium speed or a whisk, beat 5 minutes until mixture reaches a smooth consistency.

3. Add bread cubes to bowl and mix well. Pour mixture into prepared casserole dish. Sprinkle chocolate chips on top and cover dish with a lid or plastic wrap. Refrigerate overnight.

4. Preheat oven to 375°F. Uncover casserole and bake 30 minutes.

5. Remove from oven, cut into slices, place on four large plates, sprinkle with sugar, and drizzle with maple syrup.

Hummus Toast

We all love a good avocado toast, but thanks to #foodTikTok we've found new alternatives to the brunch classic, like this tasty Hummus Toast.

SERVES 2

2 cups drained canned chickpeas

2 tablespoons tahini

½ teaspoon garlic powder

¼ teaspoon kosher salt

3 tablespoons extra-virgin olive oil, divided

1 tablespoon lemon juice

2 large slices sourdough bread

⅛ teaspoon paprika

3 sprigs fresh parsley

1. In a food processor, combine chickpeas, tahini, garlic powder, salt, 2 tablespoons oil, and lemon juice. Process 5 minutes until creamy.

2. Toast bread in a toaster 5 minutes or until browned to your liking.

3. Cover one side of each toast slice with 3 tablespoons hummus. Drizzle remaining 1 tablespoon olive oil and sprinkle paprika and a few parsley leaves in the center of hummus spread. Save leftover hummus in an airtight container in the fridge up to 1 week.

Egg Lasagna

This is one of those recipes where you get to throw all of the ingredients into a dish and let the oven do all the hard work. It's a quick and delicious way of turning boring eggs into something way more flavorful and exciting.

SERVES 2

3 large eggs

⅛ teaspoon salt

¼ teaspoon ground black pepper

2 cups mozzarella cheese, divided

⅓ cup marinara sauce

¼ cup bacon bits

1. Preheat oven to 425°F. Coat a 9″ × 6″ casserole dish with nonstick cooking spray.

2. In a medium bowl, whisk together eggs with salt and pepper.

3. Add 1½ cups cheese, mixing until incorporated, and then pour mixture into prepared dish.

4. Bake 12 minutes.

5. Remove from oven and top with marinara sauce, remaining cheese, and bacon. Bake another 12 minutes.

6. Remove dish from oven and preheat broiler to high. Broil 1 minute.

7. Allow lasagna to cool 5 minutes in dish. Cut in half and serve on two small plates.

Hash Brown Waffles

A waffle maker can make more than just sweet waffles! 👁👄👁 It's time to test this tool's limits with these cheesy, protein-packed Hash Brown Waffles! Top with butter and a delicious stream of maple syrup.

SERVES 2

½ (10-ounce) bag frozen hash browns

2 medium eggs

2 tablespoons salted butter, melted

½ cup shredded mozzarella cheese

¼ teaspoon salt

⅛ teaspoon ground black pepper

1. Preheat waffle maker to medium-high heat and coat with nonstick cooking spray.

2. In a large bowl, combine all ingredients.

3. Place half of mixture in center of waffle maker and spread evenly.

4. Close waffle maker and cook 5 minutes until waffle is light brown and crispy. Place on a large plate.

5. Repeat cooking with remaining mixture.

Kitchen Hacks

Experiment with add-ins like you would with an omelet! You can add cut-up pieces of extra protein like bacon, ham, or shredded chicken to the mixture before cooking. And don't forget about veggies, like chopped onions, tomatoes, or mushrooms. You could even get saucy and drizzle a little something over the cooked waffles, like hot sauce or ranch dressing. 😋

#ForYou Tips

Share a slo-mo video of yourself drizzling maple syrup over the pancakes. Make sure to add a 🐼 to your caption and use trending music!

Panda Pancakes

This is *the* cutest way to eat pancakes—and go viral. They're just like Pancake Cereal (see recipe in this chapter), which you've seen probably a million times, but with a twist.

SERVES 1

1½ cups complete ("just add water") pancake mix

¾ cup water

1 teaspoon black food coloring

3 tablespoons maple syrup

1. In a medium bowl, whisk together pancake mix and water. Let batter rest 5 minutes.

2. Preheat a griddle to its lowest setting and coat uniformly with nonstick cooking spray.

3. Pour ¾ of batter into a squeeze bottle and set aside.

4. Add food coloring to remaining batter, mix, and pour into a second squeeze bottle.

5. Using black batter first, squeeze three small circles: two at the same level about 1½" away from each other for the eyes and a third one in between, ⅛" lower. Cook 1 minute, then use uncolored batter to squeeze and create an oval 4" in diameter that covers the black circles and creates the face of the panda.

6. Use black batter for a second time to create two ears at the two upper sides of the larger uncolored oval. If you need extra support for your hand during this process, you can use a damp cloth to rest your wrist on.

7. Once all batter layers begin to rise slightly and uncolored batter starts to turn golden at the edges, carefully flip over using a small turner spatula. Cook 45 seconds, then remove from heat and place on a large plate. Repeat with remaining batter.

8. Arrange pancakes on one large plate and drizzle with maple syrup.

Pancake Cereal

One of the best food trends of 2020 was cereal foods! Everything tastes better when it's cuter, and mini versions of things are proven to be the cutest ever.

SERVES 1

1 cup complete ("just add water") pancake mix

¾ cup water

½ tablespoon unsalted butter

2 tablespoons maple syrup

¼ cup whole milk

1. In a medium bowl, whisk together pancake mix and water. Let batter rest 5 minutes.

2. Preheat a griddle to its lowest setting and coat uniformly with nonstick cooking spray.

3. Pour batter into a squeeze bottle and make 1.5″ pancake circles on griddle.

4. Cook 1 minute, then flip pancakes. Cook another 45 seconds, then place in a medium bowl. Repeat with remaining batter.

5. Place butter on top of pancakes in middle of bowl. Drizzle with maple syrup and top with milk.

#ForYou Tips

The key to success in TikTok trends is to develop a cool twist! Experiment with different add-ins for your Pancake Cereal, like sprinkles, food coloring, crushed cookies, fruit, or candy.

Baked Avocado Eggs

Eggs are a breakfast classic, and avocados are a TikTok staple. Combine them, and you get these Baked Avocado Eggs with perfect runny egg yolks. Add crumbled cooked bacon on top for even more flavor.

SERVES 2

1 large avocado, halved and pitted

2 medium eggs

¼ teaspoon salt

¼ teaspoon ground black pepper

1. Preheat oven to 400°F.

2. Using a spoon, remove about 1 tablespoon of flesh from each avocado half to create an even bigger hole in the center. Discard removed flesh or save for another time.

3. Crack an egg over each half so yolk fills hole and sprinkle with salt and pepper.

4. Place on a small ungreased baking sheet and bake 12 minutes for a runny egg consistency or 15 minutes for a firmer yolk.

Avocado Rose Toast

Some say avocado toast is #basic, but it doesn't have to be! Up your brunch game and impress your friends and followers with this 🔥 🔥 Avocado Rose Toast. Add a few fresh flowers on top for the perfect aesthetic.

SERVES 1

1 large avocado, peeled, pitted, and thinly sliced

1 large slice sourdough bread

1 tablespoon extra-virgin olive oil

1 teaspoon lime juice

⅛ teaspoon chili flakes

⅛ teaspoon salt

1. Fan out avocado slices to form a diagonal line. Gently curl the end of the line toward itself and continue to roll to make a rose shape.

2. Toast bread to your liking and gently place the avocado rose on top. Drizzle oil and lime juice on top and sprinkle with chili flakes and salt.

Ham Biscuit Sandwiches

Another way to make good use of your waffle maker! This quick hack uses canned biscuits. It will taste better than the breakfast sandwiches you get from the drive-through, and will definitely impress your followers.

SERVES 4

1 (12-ounce) can biscuits
2 thick slices cooked ham, halved
2 slices sharp Cheddar cheese, halved

1. Preheat waffle maker to medium heat and grease with nonstick cooking spray. Separate biscuits.

2. Place 1 biscuit on center of waffle maker and top with 1 piece ham and 1 piece cheese. Place a second biscuit on top, forming a sandwich. Close waffle maker and cook 4 minutes. Repeat cooking steps to make 4 sandwiches. If your waffle maker is large enough, you can make 2 sandwiches simultaneously.

#ForYou Tips

Anything cooked with a waffle maker can make for a great #ASMR video. ASMR (autonomous sensory meridian response) is the reaction your body has to any sensation deemed as satisfying, like a crunch sound or the sizzling of a waffle maker when something cold hits its hot plates. Think about the noises that different foods make and what makes you crave them. Focus on these elements and capture them by filming in a quiet room with your phone a little bit closer to the food than usual.

Quick
and Easy
Snacks

Spicy Mozzarella Air Fryer Sticks

These are a fiery twist on the favorite drive-through snack. ✨ Make sure you keep the cheese in the fridge right up until the recipe calls for it; you want to keep it cool as long as possible. Not a fan of spicy? Swap the spicy cheese puffs for regular ones.

SERVES 4

1½ cups hot cheese puffs

1 large egg, beaten

3 tablespoons all-purpose flour

4 sticks string cheese

1. Preheat air fryer to 370°F.

2. Place cheese puffs in a food processor and blend until crumb consistency forms, about 45 seconds. Alternatively, you can put cheese puffs in a plastic bag and press down on them with a rolling pin.

3. Place puff crumbs in a medium bowl. Place egg in a second medium bowl and flour in a third medium bowl.

4. Coat a cheese stick in flour, then egg, then puff crumbs. Carefully coat once more in egg, then another layer of puff crumbs. Repeat with remaining cheese sticks.

5. Carefully place sticks in ungreased air fryer basket, making sure not to crowd them. Cook 4 minutes or until crispy on the outside and melted inside.

#For You Tips

One of the secrets to having a video go viral on TikTok is controversy. Give this recipe your own delicious controversial spin! For instance, instead of using cheese puffs, you can make your crumbs with dill pickle potato chips. Some will love the combo and others may not, but it will definitely get people talking.

Pepperoni Pizza Rolls

Anything with mozzarella cheese, pizza sauce, and pepperoni is a winning combo in my book. Seriously though, who doesn't like pizza?! Here is how to make one of the most viral snacks.

SERVES 4

1 (8-ounce) can crescent rolls

4 sticks string cheese

½ cup pizza sauce, divided

24 slices pepperoni

3 tablespoons salted butter, melted

1 teaspoon garlic powder

1 teaspoon dried parsley

1. Preheat oven to 350°F. Line a large baking sheet with parchment paper.

2. Unroll crescent roll dough, separate triangles, and lay two triangles side by side on prepared baking sheet so they form a rectangle. Press down on the edges to connect them. Repeat with remaining triangles to make four rectangles.

3. Place 1 string cheese in center of each rectangle and top with 1 tablespoon pizza sauce. Place 6 slices pepperoni on top of sauce. Repeat with remaining ingredients.

4. Fold in the shorter edges of a pizza rectangle and lightly press down, covering ends of cheese stick. Then, starting with the longer edge, roll up dough. Repeat with remaining pizza rectangles.

5. In a small bowl, combine butter, garlic powder, and parsley. Using a cooking brush, lightly brush mixture over tops of pizza rolls.

6. Bake 10 minutes or until golden brown.

7. Serve on a large plate with remaining pizza sauce on the side for dipping.

#For You Tips

This recipe is all about the cheese pull! 🐼 I have a video of myself breaking a pizza roll with both hands and trying to stretch my arms as far as I can. The cheese was so stringy that my arms weren't long enough for it! Make sure to film yourself pulling and eating a roll when posting this one.

Air Fryer Gouda Cheese

If you want to take the popular air fryer–crusted cheese up a notch and impress your friends and followers, this is how. No need for a fancy giant cheese board: This app is way easier to make and will definitely hit the spot.

SERVES 3

1 (8-ounce) can crescent rolls

1 (8-ounce) wheel Gouda cheese, room temperature

1 small egg, beaten

1 tablespoon extra-virgin olive oil

1. Preheat air fryer to 270°F. Line basket of air fryer with parchment paper.

2. Unroll crescent roll dough, making sure to keep it whole. Lay dough sheet flat on a cutting board.

3. Remove wax from cheese. Place cheese on center of dough sheet.

4. Carefully fold dough over cheese to fully wrap it. Trim excess with a knife and discard. Flip wrapped cheese over.

5. In a small bowl, whisk together egg and oil.

6. Using a brush, cover top of wrapped Gouda with egg wash, making sure to get all edges.

7. Place cheese on ungreased parchment and cook 12 minutes or until crust is golden and cheese is melted.

8. Serve on a medium plate and eat immediately with a fork.

Garlic Turtle Bread

Sourdough is all the talk, and I get why: It's delicious! Sure, viewers love it as is, but here's how to turn it into a mind-blowing cheesy app that looks like a turtle's shell.

SERVES 4

1 round loaf sourdough bread

¼ cup salted butter, melted

1 teaspoon garlic powder

¼ teaspoon onion powder

½ teaspoon dried parsley

⅛ teaspoon ground black pepper

5 sticks string cheese, cut into quarters

¾ cup shredded mozzarella cheese

¼ cup grated Parmesan cheese

1. Preheat oven to 400°F. Line a large baking sheet with parchment paper.

2. With a serrated knife, make a series of vertical cuts halfway through bread every 2″. Turn bread 180° and repeat cuts to make a crosshatch pattern.

3. Place bread on prepared baking sheet.

4. In a small bowl, whisk together butter, garlic powder, onion powder, parsley, and pepper.

5. Using a brush, lightly coat top of bread with butter mixture.

6. Stuff gaps in bread with string cheese pieces, pushing down with your fingers. Top with shredded mozzarella and lightly push down. Repeat process with Parmesan.

7. Bake 8 minutes until cheese is melted and begins to crisp.

8. Serve on a large plate. Pull apart pieces with your fingers.

Air Fryer Banana Bread

Banana bread is one of those 2020 recipes you felt like everyone and their moms were making. My one problem with it is that it takes forever to bake, and I want to be eating it now. But guess what? Air fryers cut baking time in half! No more waiting around for that deliciousness.

SERVES 4

3 large ripe bananas, peeled and mashed

2 medium eggs

5 tablespoons canola oil

1 teaspoon vanilla extract

1 cup all-purpose flour

1 cup granulated sugar

½ tablespoon baking soda

1 tablespoon kosher salt

½ (1.7-ounce) packet instant vanilla pudding

1 (1.5-ounce) bar milk chocolate, sliced into long, thin pieces

1. Preheat air fryer to 350°F. Grease a 5″ Bundt or loaf pan with nonstick cooking spray.

2. In a large bowl, combine bananas, eggs, oil, and vanilla.

3. In a separate medium bowl, combine all dry ingredients using a whisk.

4. Add dry ingredients to bowl with bananas and whisk together by hand. Add chocolate pieces to batter and combine.

5. Pour batter into greased pan, then place in air fryer basket. Cook 20 minutes or until brown and a toothpick inserted in center comes out clean.

6. Let cool at least 20 minutes before serving. Cut with a serrated knife.

Kitchen Hacks

Don't be afraid to bake using your air fryer! You can follow basically any baking recipe in the air fryer, and it will turn out just as good—and take less time to bake. When following the instructions of a traditional recipe in your air fryer, make sure to lower the temperature by 30°F and decrease the cooking time by around 20 percent.

Two-Ingredient Bagels

Fresh bagels are actually supereasy to make and are the perfect breakfast or snack! You can make all kinds of bagel flavors and versions with this recipe. Sprinkle cinnamon on the dough and add some light brown sugar, and you've got a sweet bagel. Don't have self-rising flour? Just use 2 cups all-purpose flour combined with 1 tablespoon baking powder and ½ teaspoon salt!

MAKES 8 BAGELS

For Bagels

2 cups self-rising flour, plus extra
   for work surface

1 cup plain Greek yogurt

For Topping

1 large egg

1 tablespoon water

2 tablespoons Everything Bagel seasoning

1. Preheat air fryer to 350°F. Line air fryer basket with parchment paper.

2. In a large bowl, combine 2 cups flour and yogurt. Empty dough onto a lightly floured work surface and begin to knead with your hands. If dough is too dry, add extra yogurt; if it's too wet, add more flour.

3. Once you have a smooth dough ball, separate dough into eight equal pieces. Make a ball out of each piece, and use your thumbs to make a hole in the center of each. Flatten slightly to create a bagel shape.

4. Place four bagels in prepared air fryer basket. Make sure to not crowd basket.

5. In a small bowl, whisk together egg and water. Brush over tops of bagels and sprinkle with seasoning.

6. Cook 12 minutes. Allow to cool 5 minutes before serving. Repeat with remaining bagels.

To make an egg wash to brush over bagels, croissants, pies, and any baked good in need of a nice golden color, mix together 1 egg and 1 tablespoon water.

Kitchen Hacks

Pizza in a Mug

You've probably seen tons of "in a mug" microwavable desserts, but what about some savory treats, please?? Give yourself (and your viewers) what you deserve with this easy Pizza in a Mug!

SERVES 1

8 Ritz crackers

1½ tablespoons pizza sauce

⅓ tablespoon unsalted butter, melted

⅓ cup shredded mozzarella cheese, divided

1 tablespoon mini pepperoni slices

1. Spray inside of a large microwave-safe mug with nonstick cooking spray. Add crackers, then sauce and butter. Using a fork, mash ingredients together and mix.

2. Set aside 2 tablespoons cheese and sprinkle the rest on top of cracker mixture. Mix together, then sprinkle remaining cheese on top. Top with pepperoni slices.

3. Microwave mug on medium-high 2 minutes.

4. Let cool 3 minutes before eating with a fork.

#For You Tips

This is one of those creations that is extremely polarizing—and that's why I recommend you post it on TikTok! Why? Well, a lot of people will have strong opinions about it and flood your comments. That's the key to success on social media ✨ engagement, ✨ and this dish is guaranteed to provide you with just that. Make sure your replies to the comments are kind; don't let any Internet trolls get to you!

Garden Focaccia

Sourdough was a major 2020 trend, but focaccia is way easier to make and super-customizable! By placing tomatoes, peppers, and herbs on top, you can make a fairy-tale bread viewers will love. Try different peppers, swap the tomatoes for olives, or experiment with onion "blooms." For the leaves and stems, try parsley or oregano instead of the chives, rosemary, and basil if you prefer.

SERVES 6

1½ cups 100°F water

1 tablespoon active dry yeast

2 teaspoons granulated sugar

3½ cups 00 flour, divided

6 tablespoons extra-virgin olive oil, divided

1½ teaspoons kosher salt

4 medium grape tomatoes, halved

2 mini sweet peppers, sliced and seeded

½ ounce whole fresh chives

3 sprigs fresh rosemary

10 leaves fresh basil (including stem)

1. Place water in a medium bowl. Add yeast and sugar and mix together. Let sit 10 minutes or until a foam begins to form and rise to the top.

2. Add half of flour to bowl of a stand mixer and pour in yeast mixture and 3 tablespoons oil. Beat at medium-low speed using flat beater 1 minute. Add remaining flour and continue to beat at medium-low speed 3 more minutes, stopping once or twice to scrape edges of bowl using a spatula. Dough should be slightly sticky and come off beater easily; if it doesn't, add ¼ cup flour and mix.

3. Grease a 9″ × 13″ baking dish with 1 tablespoon oil. Place dough in dish and flatten. Cover with a cloth and let rest 1 hour somewhere warm. Dough should double in size. Flatten once again and poke holes with your fingertips.

4. Preheat oven to 400°F. Brush surface of dough with remaining oil and sprinkle with salt. Scatter tomato halves (cut-side down) and pepper slices, and place chives under them to form flower stems. Scatter rosemary sprigs and basil leaves across top.

5. Bake 20 minutes until light golden. Let rest 10 minutes before cutting.

Kitchen Hacks

Finding Italian 00 flour may be a little bit tricky: It's mostly sold in specialty stores. It's the same kind of flour used in Neapolitan pizza and other traditional Italian recipes such as pasta. What makes this flour special is how finely ground it is—it's the finest grind you can find. 👁👁👁 You can use all-purpose flour instead if you don't have 00 flour on hand.

Cloud Bread

This is one of the most random recipes to go viral on TikTok, thanks to the keto diet. Picture a light, jiggly, cloudlike bread with the texture of an airy soufflé. When making your own version, feel free to switch out the vanilla extract for any other flavor, like almond, lemon, or orange extract. You can also add some food coloring for a more whimsical-looking cloud, and top it off with sprinkles, sliced nuts, or chocolate chips.

SERVES 1

3 medium egg whites, room temperature

1 teaspoon vanilla extract

1½ tablespoons cornstarch

2 tablespoons granulated sugar

1. Preheat oven to 300°F. Line a small baking sheet with parchment paper.

2. Add egg whites and vanilla to a medium bowl. Using an electric mixer set to medium-high speed or a whisk, beat about 3 minutes until soft peaks form.

3. Add cornstarch to egg whites and combine with a spatula. Add sugar and mix in with same spatula.

4. Spoon ⅓ egg white mixture into center of prepared baking sheet. Top with another ⅓, followed by remaining ⅓. Using edge of spatula, shape mixture into a dome.

5. Bake 20 minutes until fluffy and golden on outside.

6. Remove from oven and cool 2 minutes, then break down the middle with your hands.

#For You Tips

To get the perfect #foodporn Cloud Bread shot, break the bread in half almost immediately after getting it out of the oven. It flattens superquickly, so you want to showcase it at its jiggliest moment.

Muffin Cereal

Pancake Cereal (see recipe in Chapter 3) was a total cultural reset during 2020 and the rise of TikTok. It started the trend of making mini versions of every food possible. One of the cutest *and* tastiest takes on this trend is Muffin Cereal!

SERVES 4

2 cups all-purpose flour

3 teaspoons baking powder

1 cup granulated sugar

3 tablespoons canola oil

¼ teaspoon salt

1 medium egg

1¼ cups whole milk, divided

⅓ cup mini milk chocolate chips

1. Preheat oven to 400°F. Grease a silicone mold with thirty-five cavities intended for chocolate making with nonstick cooking spray. Alternatively, you can use a mini-muffin tin.

2. In a large bowl, whisk together flour, baking powder, sugar, oil, salt, egg, and 1 cup milk.

3. Add batter to a piping bag and cut a tip to make a 1″ hole. Pipe into each cavity/mini-muffin cup.

4. Sprinkle even amounts of chocolate chips over each cavity/mini-muffin cup and bake 8 minutes.

5. Remove from oven and let cool 5 minutes. Release muffins and divide among four cereal bowls. Pour remaining milk on top and eat with a spoon.

Ice Cream Bread

Here's another supercool hack for you: Bread can be made without yeast! This recipe uses ingredients you probably already have, and makes a rich, buttery, cakelike bread. Don't have self-rising flour? Use 1¼ cups all-purpose flour mixed with 1½ teaspoons baking powder and ⅛ teaspoon salt.

SERVES 6

2 cups melted vanilla ice cream
1¼ cups self-rising flour

1. Preheat oven to 350°F. Grease a 9" × 5" loaf pan with nonstick cooking spray.

2. In a large bowl, combine ice cream and flour using a spatula or dough whisk.

3. Pour batter into prepared pan. Hold with both hands and tap hard against a sturdy flat surface to get rid of any air bubbles.

4. Bake 35 minutes.

5. Remove from oven and let cool 15 minutes. Cut into six 1½" slices with a serrated knife.

Kitchen Hacks

Vanilla not your thing? Swap it out for any of your favorite flavors (or whatever's in the freezer ATM). It can be something simple like chocolate or something a little more #EXTRA ✨ like cotton candy or rocky road.

Mini Pepperoni Pizza Waffles

Don't sleep on savory waffles! I repeat: Don't sleep on savory waffles! They're *sooo* easy to make and are a delicious snack. Waffle makers can be a superversatile tool if you set your mind to it.

SERVES 4

1½ cups complete ("just add water") pancake mix

¾ cup water

½ cup grated Parmesan cheese

½ teaspoon Italian seasoning

⅛ teaspoon salt

1 cup shredded mozzarella cheese

⅓ cup mini pepperoni slices

½ cup marinara sauce

1. In a medium bowl, whisk together pancake mix and water. Let batter rest 5 minutes.

2. Preheat waffle maker to medium-high heat.

3. In a large bowl, combine pancake batter with Parmesan, Italian seasoning, and salt using a whisk or spatula.

4. Spray waffle maker with nonstick cooking spray and pour in ¼ cup batter. Top with 2 tablespoons mozzarella cheese. Pour 2 more tablespoons batter over cheese. Place a few pepperoni slices on top and close waffle maker.

5. Cook waffle 4 minutes, then place on a large plate. Repeat with remaining ingredients.

6. Serve with marinara sauce on the side for dipping.

Crusted Round Cheese

Mozzarella sticks are a classic, but what if you don't have string cheese? Or want to switch things up? You use round mini Dutch cheeses: They have a supermilky, delicious taste!

SERVES 6

1½ cups nacho cheese–flavored tortilla chips
1 large egg, beaten
3 tablespoons all-purpose flour
6 mini rounds Dutch Edam cheese, cold

1. Preheat air fryer to 370°F.

2. Place tortilla chips in a food processor and blend to crumb consistency, about 30 seconds. Alternatively, you can place chips in a large plastic bag and press down with a rolling pin.

3. Add tortilla crumbs to a medium bowl, egg to a second medium bowl, and flour to a third medium bowl. Remove cheese from wax packaging.

4. Coat 1 cheese round in flour, then egg, ensuring edges are fully covered. Next, coat in crumbs. Carefully coat a second time in egg, then again in crumbs. Repeat with remaining cheese rounds.

5. Carefully place cheese rounds in ungreased air fryer basket, making sure not to crowd them. Cook 4 minutes until crispy on outside and melted inside.

6. Place on a large plate and let cool 2 minutes before breaking apart with your hands.

Cinnamon Roll in a Mug

I like to challenge the limits of what can be cooked in a mug. Brownies, cookies, and cakes are easy, but have you ever heard of a Cinnamon Roll in a Mug?! This is the most elite mug recipe.

SERVES 3

1 medium egg

1 tablespoon granulated sugar

3 tablespoons whole milk, divided

1 tablespoon vanilla extract

1½ cups complete ("just add water") pancake mix

1½ tablespoons all-purpose flour

1 tablespoon unsalted butter, melted

2 tablespoons dark brown sugar

½ teaspoon ground cinnamon

1 teaspoon water

4 tablespoons powdered sugar

1. In a medium bowl, whisk together egg, granulated sugar, 2 tablespoons milk, and vanilla. Add pancake mix and combine.

2. Use flour to coat a flat surface, and empty dough onto flour. Knead dough until smooth. Flatten and create an 8" × 6" rectangle. Trim edges using a knife to create straight lines.

3. In a small bowl, combine butter, brown sugar, and cinnamon. Spread evenly over dough using a spatula.

4. Roll dough into a log and cut into three even pieces.

5. Place one roll in a large mug. Sprinkle water on top of roll, and microwave at 50 percent power 1 minute and 45 seconds.

6. Repeat with remaining rolls and two more large mugs. Let mugs cool 3 minutes.

7. In a small bowl, whisk together powdered sugar and remaining milk. Drizzle over cooled rolls and eat with a spoon.

Pull-Apart Garlic Roll Cups

All forms of cheese, bread, and, best of all, cheesy bread, are delicious. But garlic cheesy bread has a special place in my heart: There is *nothing* more comforting. This is an awesome recipe to share with your audience—it's easy to make, but superindulgent.

SERVES 8

1 (16-ounce) can large butter biscuits

¼ tablespoon unsalted butter, melted

½ teaspoon garlic powder

½ teaspoon dried parsley

2 cups shredded mozzarella cheese

1. Preheat oven to 375°F. Coat eight cups of a twelve-cup muffin tin with nonstick cooking spray.

2. Separate eight biscuits and cut each into quarters.

3. In a large bowl, combine butter, garlic powder, and parsley. Toss in biscuit quarters and coat.

4. Place two biscuit dough quarters in the bottom of one muffin cup and press down with your fingers. Add ¼ cup mozzarella and cover with two more biscuit quarters, pressing down. Repeat to fill eight cups.

5. Bake 15 minutes.

6. Let cool 10 minutes before removing from tin.

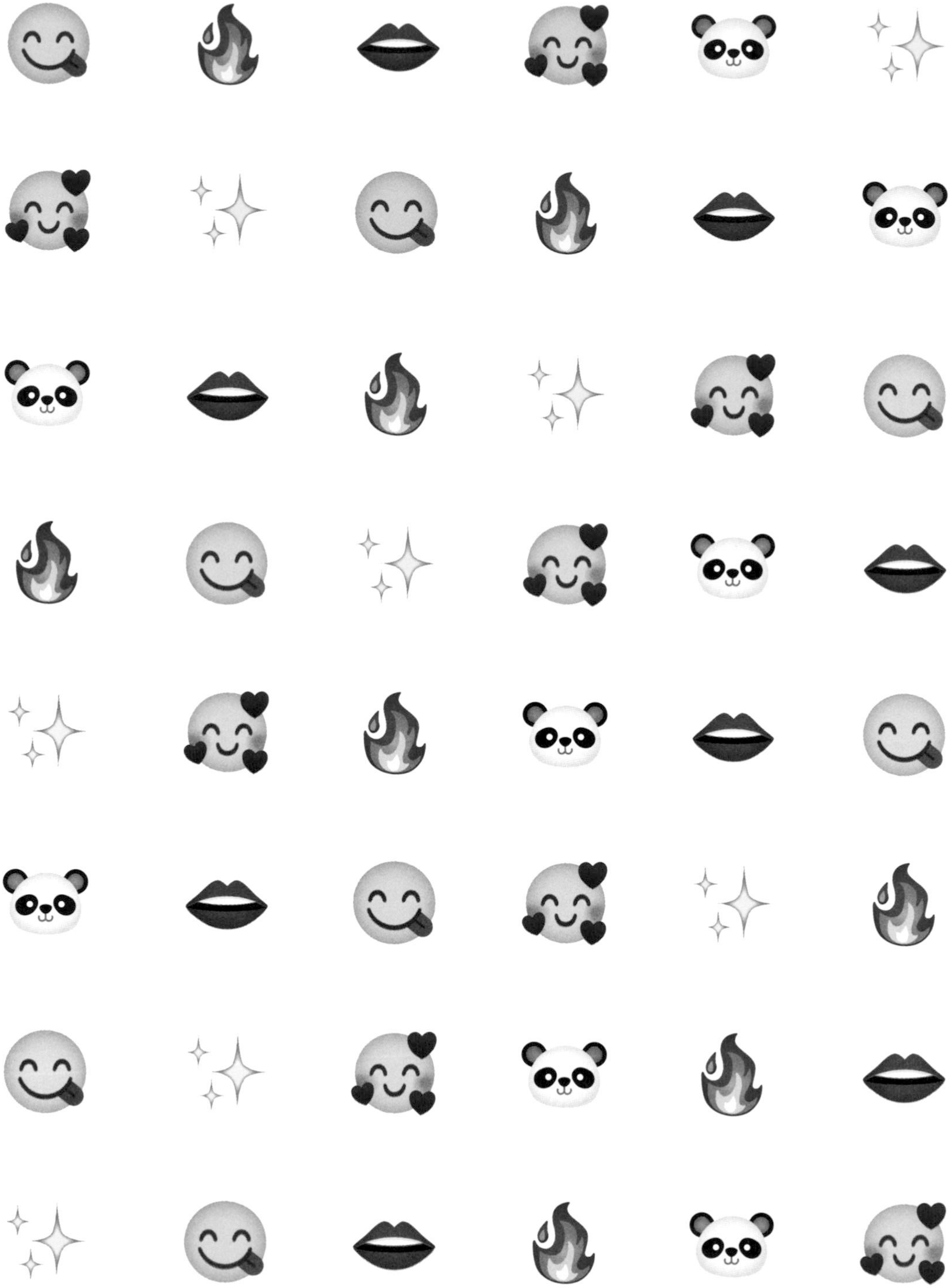

Lunch and Dinner

Upgraded Ramen Noodles

Ramen noodles are the ultimate cheap eat, but they get boring fast. Here's a supereasy glow-up to turn them into an impressive meal worth sharing.

SERVES 1

1 medium egg

1 (3-ounce) package uncooked chicken ramen

1 medium clove garlic, peeled and minced

¼ cup heavy cream

3 tablespoons sriracha

1. Fill a small saucepan ¾ full with water and bring to a boil over high heat. Carefully place egg in pan and boil 6 minutes.

2. While egg cooks, fill a small bowl with ice and water. Using a slotted spoon, remove cooked egg and carefully place in cold water.

3. Once cool enough to touch, about 3 minutes, peel egg and cut in half.

4. Rinse out saucepan and bring 2 cups water to a boil over high heat. Add ramen seasoning packets. Mix well with a fork.

5. Add ramen noodles to saucepan and cook 2 minutes.

6. Lower heat to medium-low and add garlic, cream, and sriracha. Stir and cook 3 more minutes.

7. Serve noodles in a medium bowl topped with soft-boiled egg.

#ForYou Tips

Move over #CheesePull, here comes #NoodlePull! A noodle pull is when you take chopsticks, grab as many noodles as you possibly can, and lift them up as high as your arm can go. This is a great way to show off the dish and get beauty shots after you're done cooking.

Cheese-Stuffed Meatballs

Everything is better stuffed with cheese! You can eat these delicious meatballs on their own, in a provolone cheese sandwich, or on top of spaghetti.

SERVES 6

1 pound 85% lean ground beef

1 medium egg

⅓ cup Italian bread crumbs

1 tablespoon Italian seasoning

1 teaspoon salt

1 teaspoon garlic powder

4 sticks string cheese, quartered

3 tablespoons vegetable oil

1. In a large bowl, combine all ingredients except cheese and oil using your hands.

2. Roll 1½ tablespoons meat mixture into a ball. Press down lightly, creating a cavity for cheese. Place 1 piece cheese in cavity and push meat up to cover cheese and reshape into a ball. Repeat with remaining meat and cheese pieces.

3. In a large pan, add oil and cook meatballs over medium heat 15 minutes or until fully cooked on inside and crispy on outside. Use tongs to turn meatballs during cooking to ensure each side is cooked.

4. Move meatballs to a large plate to cool 3 minutes before serving.

Cheesy Tortellini with Pancetta

This is the cheesiest pasta guaranteed to get you the perfect cheese-pull shot. It's also easy to make, and great for #DateNight or dinner with friends.

SERVES 4

1 pound uncooked three-cheese tortellini

4 tablespoons unsalted butter

½ cup diced pancetta

1½ cups heavy cream

¼ teaspoon salt

¼ teaspoon ground black pepper

4 ounces fresh mozzarella cheese balls, quartered

¼ cup grated Parmigiano-Reggiano cheese

1. Fill a large pot about ¾ full with water and bring to a boil over high heat. Add tortellini and cook 4 minutes. Strain, reserving 1 cup cooking water.

2. In a large skillet over medium heat, melt butter, then add pancetta. Cook 5 minutes until light brown and slightly crispy.

3. Slowly add cream, season with salt and pepper, and cook over medium-low heat 5 minutes, allowing it to simmer.

4. Add cooked tortellini to skillet with sauce and, using tongs, continuously flip to coat. Mix in mozzarella.

5. Cook 3 more minutes, allowing mozzarella to melt. If sauce is looking dry, add a bit of reserved cooking water.

6. Serve on a large plate with Parmesan sprinkled on top.

#ForYou Tips

There are two tricks to getting the perfect cheese-pull shot with this recipe. The first is to wait! I know, I know—it's tricky to do, especially when you've got a big plate of deliciousness sitting right in front of you. But cheese becomes stringier if you let it sit for 2–3 minutes. The second trick is to have your phone ready. If you aren't ready to snap a pic and you've already lifted your fork, all you've got is a #fail. Have your phone open to the camera first, lift your fork, and get that perfect shot of the cheese pull.

Taco Calzone

This is a Mexican take on the calzone. Maybe it sounds kind of crazy, but it is supereasy to create and will impress your #TacoTuesday guests.

SERVES 2

1 tablespoon vegetable oil

½ pound 90% lean ground beef

1 tablespoon taco seasoning

½ teaspoon salt

1 (14-ounce) can premade pizza dough

1 cup seasoned black beans

1½ cups mild salsa, divided

1 cup Mexican blend shredded cheese

2 tablespoons unsalted butter, melted

1. Preheat oven to 375°F. Line a large baking sheet with parchment paper.

2. In a medium skillet over medium-high heat, heat oil 30 seconds, then add beef, taco seasoning, and salt. Combine and cook 8 minutes until fully cooked and slightly crispy.

3. Unroll dough over prepared baking sheet.

4. Scatter beans over half of dough. Over same half, add beef, ½ cup salsa, and cheese.

5. Carefully lift other half of dough and fold over beef mixture. Crimp edges by pressing down along them with a fork.

6. Brush calzone with butter.

7. Bake 13 minutes until deep golden brown.

8. Remove from oven and let sit 5 minutes before cutting in half. Serve remaining salsa on the side for dipping.

Fried Mozzarella Burger

Cheeseburgers are good. But you want to know what's even better? A cheeseburger with fried mozzarella instead of boring yellow cheese. Bet you've never had anything like this before!

SERVES 1

1 (¼-pound) burger patty

¼ teaspoon salt

⅛ teaspoon ground black pepper

2 tablespoons all-purpose flour

1 large egg, beaten

4 tablespoons plain bread crumbs

1 slice mozzarella cheese

1 brioche burger bun

1 tablespoon Dijon mustard

½ small Roma tomato, sliced

½ cup fresh arugula

1. Preheat a griddle to medium-high heat and coat with nonstick cooking spray. Season burger patty on both sides with salt and pepper. Cook patty 4 minutes per side.

2. Preheat air fryer to 370°F.

3. Place flour in a medium bowl, egg in a second medium bowl, and bread crumbs in a third medium bowl.

4. Coat cheese in flour, dip in egg, and then coat in bread crumbs. Dip in egg again and coat once more in bread crumbs.

5. Place coated mozzarella in ungreased air fryer basket and cook 4 minutes.

6. Toast bun in oven or toaster to your liking.

7. With a spoon, spread mustard on bottom bun. Place patty on top, followed by fried cheese. Top with tomato slices, arugula, and bun lid.

Spicy Cheese Puff–Crusted Chicken Tenders

These chicken tenders are *sooo* easy to make and are perfectly cooked in the air fryer. The bright red color of the cheese puff crust will amaze your followers.

SERVES 4

2 cups hot cheese puffs

½ cup plain bread crumbs

¼ cup all-purpose flour

2 large eggs, beaten

8 (2-ounce) chicken tenders

1 teaspoon kosher salt

1 teaspoon paprika

½ teaspoon garlic powder

1. Preheat air fryer to 370°F.

2. Using a food processor or plastic bag and rolling pin, crush cheese puffs to a crumb consistency. Pour in a medium bowl, add bread crumbs, and mix together.

3. Add flour to a separate medium bowl. Add eggs to a third medium bowl.

4. Place chicken tenders in a large bowl and rub in salt, paprika, and garlic powder on all sides.

5. Coat each chicken tender in flour and then dip in egg. Shake off excess egg and coat in crumb mixture.

6. Place tenders in ungreased air fryer basket without overlapping and fry 7 minutes. Flip over and fry another 7 minutes.

Don't have an air fryer? Just bake the chicken tenders at 400°F for 18 minutes per side. I've got ya, boo! 😋

Kitchen Hacks

French Onion Soup in a Bread Bowl

This is not a regular soup: This is a total soup glow-up! No boring canned soups or plain bowls (and bowl cleanup) here.

SERVES 2

3½ tablespoons extra-virgin olive oil, divided

2 small yellow onions, peeled and julienned

2 teaspoons salt

1 teaspoon ground black pepper

4 tablespoons unsalted butter

½ teaspoon granulated sugar

4 cups beef stock

½ cup red cooking wine

2 cups water

2 round loaves sourdough bread

2 cups grated Gruyère cheese

1. In a large skillet over medium heat, add 2 tablespoons oil, then add onions. Cook 10 minutes while stirring until onions begin to soften and look transparent.

2. Season onions with salt and pepper. While still stirring, add butter and sugar. Increase heat to medium-high and cook 10 more minutes, stirring occasionally.

3. Add stock, wine, and water. Cook until mixture boils, then reduce heat to low and simmer 15 minutes. If soup is too thin, add 1 tablespoon flour to a small mug, dissolve in ½ cup water, and pour into soup while stirring.

4. Preheat oven to 400°F. Using a serrated knife, carve out a 3"-deep hole in the center of each bread loaf that is 5" wide.

5. Using a brush, coat inside of bread bowls and 3" x 5" "lids" with remaining oil. Place bowls and lids on a baking tray lined with parchment paper and bake 8 minutes until toasted. Remove from oven.

6. Preheat oven to broil on high.

7. Ladle 1½ cups soup into each bowl and top with 1 cup cheese, then lids. Broil on a large unlined baking sheet 2 minutes until cheese is fully melted and beginning to crisp.

8. Remove bread bowls from oven and serve on medium plates with spoons.

Skillet Pizza Mac 'n' Cheese

Everything tastes better in a cast iron skillet—these are facts! Here's how to take boxed macaroni to the next level with your favorite pizza flavors.

SERVES 4

1 (7-ounce) box mac 'n' cheese
1 cup heavy cream
½ teaspoon salt
¼ teaspoon ground black pepper
3 cups shredded mozzarella cheese, divided
¼ cup pepperoni slices

1. Preheat oven to 400°F. Coat a 12″ cast iron skillet with nonstick cooking spray.

2. In a medium pot over high heat, cook mac 'n' cheese according to package instructions (leaving out cheese packet).

3. Drain, then add pasta back to pot over medium heat. Add in cream, salt, and pepper, and stir until cream is heated, about 4 minutes.

4. Add 2 cups mozzarella and stir until fully melted.

5. Pour mixture into prepared skillet and top with remaining mozzarella. Sprinkle pepperoni on top.

6. Bake 15 minutes until cheese on top is a deep golden brown color.

7. Serve on four large plates.

Aligot

Mashed potatoes, meet melty fondue cheese. This is the ultimate potato side dish: cheesy, stretchy, and so comforting. Here is how to make the Insta-famous French dish at home.

SERVES 4

3 tablespoons sea salt

4 medium golden potatoes, peeled and quartered

4 medium cloves garlic, peeled

½ cup unsalted butter, chilled, cut into 6 pieces

½ cup heavy cream, heated

½ pound French Comté cheese, rind removed, grated

1. Fill a large pot about ¾ full with water, add salt, and bring to a boil over medium-high heat. Add potatoes and garlic and simmer 20 minutes until potatoes are tender.

2. Drain water and discard garlic. Immediately push hot potatoes through a ricer or strainer using a wooden spoon.

3. Place mashed potatoes back into pot and cook over low heat while mixing with a wooden spoon 3 minutes.

4. Add cold butter pieces 1 at a time and mix until fully melted and incorporated. Slowly add cream, stirring until incorporated.

5. Add cheese a little at a time while vigorously stirring until melted and incorporated.

Kitchen Hacks

Serve this immediately on a small plate or as a side dish. Aligot is very stringy, so you might want to get a spoonful, lift, and cut the string with scissors (the cheese string won't break on its own as you keep pulling). If you've got leftovers, the cheese will harden in the fridge, so reheat the dish in the microwave or in a pan over medium-low heat to remelt the cheese and get that original texture back.

Rolled Lasagna

These lasagna pinwheels are superaesthetic and became famous at Don Angie restaurant in New York. As much as we'd love to fly to NYC just to have them, it's not exactly an option for most of us ATM (or ever). Luckily, they're easy to make at home!

SERVES 6

3 tablespoons sea salt

6 uncooked lasagna noodles

2 cups ricotta cheese

3 cups Bolognese sauce

4 cups shredded mozzarella cheese, divided

1. Preheat oven to 350°F. Grease an 8″ × 8″ baking pan with nonstick cooking spray.

2. Fill a large pot about ¾ full with water, add salt, and bring to a boil over high heat. Add lasagna noodles and cook following package instructions.

3. Drain noodles and lay flat on a cutting board. Using a spatula, spread ⅓ cup ricotta over each noodle. Using a spoon, add ½ cup sauce on top of each and spread. Sprinkle ⅓ cup mozzarella on top of each.

4. Carefully roll each lasagna noodle starting at one long end. Place in prepared pan with rolled side facing up. Sprinkle remaining mozzarella on top.

5. Bake 25 minutes until cheese is fully melted and top is a deep golden brown.

6. Serve each roll on a small plate.

Tortilla Enchiladas

#TacoTuesday is one of the best days of the week, but ordering the same tacos gets old. Here's how to switch things up *and* bring casseroles into the TikTok era.

SERVES 6

1 tablespoon extra-virgin olive oil

1 pound 90% lean ground beef

2 tablespoons taco seasoning

1 (11-ounce) bag tortilla chips

1 (14-ounce) can enchilada sauce

1 (16-ounce) can seasoned pinto beans, drained

5 cups shredded Mexican blend cheese

1. Preheat oven to 375°F.

2. In a medium skillet over medium heat, add oil. Add beef, seasoning, and cook 9 minutes, stirring occasionally, until brown and slightly crispy.

3. Add half of tortilla chips to an ungreased 9" × 12" casserole dish. Spread chips evenly.

4. Add half of beef evenly over chips. Layer half of sauce on top, followed by half of beans. Sprinkle 1½ cups cheese evenly on top. Repeat with remaining ingredients.

5. Cover dish with aluminum foil and bake 15 minutes. Remove foil and bake another 10 minutes.

6. Serve on six large plates.

Chicken Teriyaki Pineapple Bowls

Have you seen the amazing pics all over Instagram of food served in pineapple bowls? Well, it's time to bring this trend to TikTok and teach your audience how to re-create it at home!

SERVES 2

1 large pineapple, halved lengthwise, stem on

4 cups vegetable oil

½ cup all-purpose flour

½ cup + 1 tablespoon cornstarch, divided

2 large eggs, beaten

2 (5-ounce) chicken breasts, diced

1 cup water

⅓ cup soy sauce

1 tablespoon honey

¼ cup dark brown sugar

1 teaspoon ground ginger

2 cups cooked white rice

½ teaspoon sesame seeds

1. Remove core and flesh of each pineapple half using a spoon. You can save flesh for another time or discard.

2. Heat oil in a large saucepan over medium-high heat until it reaches 350°F.

3. In a large bowl, combine flour and ½ cup cornstarch. Add eggs to a separate medium bowl.

4. Using tongs, toss chicken in egg and fully coat. Coat in flour mixture.

5. Drop chicken in oil and cook 4 minutes per side or until golden and reaches a minimum internal temperature of 165°F. Remove chicken from oil, rest 2 minutes on a large plate, then pat dry with paper towel.

6. In a small saucepan over medium-high heat, make teriyaki sauce by combining water, soy sauce, honey, sugar, and ginger. Once sauce begins to bubble up after 6 minutes, lower heat to a simmer and add remaining cornstarch. Stir continuously until sauce thickens, about 5 minutes.

7. In a large bowl, toss chicken in teriyaki sauce to fully coat.

8. Add 1 cup rice to each pineapple half, followed by half of cooked chicken. Sprinkle ¼ teaspoon sesame seeds over each bowl.

Honeycomb Pasta Cake

Baked ziti is good, but a pasta cake that looks like honeycomb? Even better (and way cooler looking)! This is one of my mom's favorite dishes to make, and now I'm bringing you in on the family recipe!

SERVES 5

¾ pound uncooked rigatoni pasta

5 cups Bolognese sauce

3 cups shredded mozzarella cheese

1 cup grated Parmigiano-Reggiano cheese

1. Preheat oven to 380°F.

2. Cook pasta al dente following package instructions. Strain.

3. Grease bottom and sides of a 9″ springform pan with butter. Stand rigatoni noodles on end, one next to another, until pan is filled.

4. Using a ladle, pour sauce over pasta to fill holes. Sprinkle mozzarella on top to fill holes and gaps in an even layer. Evenly sprinkle Parmigiano-Reggiano on top.

5. Cover pan with aluminum foil and bake 20 minutes. Remove foil and bake another 10 minutes.

6. Remove pan from oven and let cool 10 minutes before removing sides of pan. Cut lasagna into fifths and lift out onto small plates with a serving spatula.

Mac 'n' Cheese Pizza

This is one of those recipes that uses simple store-bought ingredients for a quick, tasty meal. It's not the fanciest pizza you will ever eat, but it's for sure the one that will satisfy all your carb cravings.

SERVES 4

1 (12-ounce) can pizza dough

2 cups cooked mac 'n' cheese

3 cups shredded mozzarella cheese

½ cup pepperoni slices

1. Preheat oven to 400°F. Line a large baking sheet with parchment paper.

2. Unroll dough on prepared baking sheet to form a crust.

3. Using a spatula, spread mac 'n' cheese on dough, then sprinkle with mozzarella on top. Top off with pepperoni slices.

4. Bake 15 minutes.

5. Remove from oven. Using a pizza cutter, cut into 3″ squares. Eat while still hot.

#ForYou Tips

This recipe proves that you can use pretty much anything as a pizza topping. 👀🍝👀 TikTok cooking is all about bending the "rules" and making dishes that you probably won't see at a restaurant. So what's next? Spaghetti and meatballs? Taco filling? You show me!

CHAPTER 6

Desserts, Desserts, and More Desserts

Birthday Mug Cake

Forgot to get your friend a birthday cake? Here's how to make a mini version in less than 5 minutes using your microwave! It's just as good and spongy as an actual cake; all that's missing is a candle on top.

SERVES 1

½ cup all-purpose flour

¼ teaspoon baking powder

4 tablespoons granulated sugar

1½ tablespoons unsalted butter, melted

5 tablespoons whole milk

⅛ teaspoon vanilla extract

2 teaspoons rainbow sprinkles, divided

Canned whipped cream

1. In a large microwave-safe mug, combine flour, baking powder, and sugar.

2. Add butter, milk, vanilla, and 1 teaspoon sprinkles and stir.

3. Microwave on high 1 minute. Let cool 5 minutes.

4. Add a big swirl of whipped cream on top, followed by remaining sprinkles. Eat with a fork or spoon.

Hazelnut Spread French Toast

French toast is my go-to brunch food, but it can get a little boring. So here's how to make the most scrumptious chocolatey French toast that will get you all the likes!

SERVES 4

½ loaf brioche bread, cut into 4
    (3"-thick) slices

½ cup hazelnut spread

2 medium eggs

1 (7-ounce) can evaporated milk

1 (7-ounce) can sweetened
    condensed milk

3 tablespoons unsalted butter

2 tablespoons powdered sugar

1. Carefully slice along one edge of each bread slice, creating a 2"-deep slit.

2. Add hazelnut spread to a piping bag or large plastic bag. Cut a tip 1½" wide and pipe 2 tablespoons hazelnut spread inside hole of each bread slice.

3. In a medium bowl, whisk together eggs, evaporated milk, and condensed milk. Dip bread slices into mixture, making sure to cover both sides.

4. Preheat a large griddle greased with butter to medium-high heat. Place slices on griddle and cook 1½ minutes per side.

5. Serve on a large plate topped with sugar.

Kitchen Hacks

You can use this same technique to make all kinds of stuffed French toast flavors. Instead of hazelnut spread, try cookie butter, peanut butter, or dulce de leche. Of course, you're not stuck with thick spreads: You can use any kind of jam, frosting, or whipped cream! 😊

Mason Jar Ice Cream

Ever make ice cream using this method as a kid? It's the best way of making it at home without any extra equipment—no ice cream machine, no mixer—just a jar and some shaking for a supercreamy treat. Don't have a jar? You can use a sealed plastic food container with a tight lid instead.

SERVES 2

2 cups heavy cream
¼ cup granulated sugar
2 tablespoons vanilla extract
⅛ teaspoon salt

1. Add all ingredients to a large Mason jar and close lid tightly.

2. Shake jar at least 5 minutes. You will see it begin to thicken, and cream will begin to form stiff peaks. Stop shaking once a thick consistency reminiscent of whipped cream is reached.

3. Place jar in freezer and freeze at least 3 hours.

4. Open lid and spoon into two small bowls to serve. Ice cream will keep in freezer up to 1 week.

Chocolate Waffle Tacos

#TacoTuesday isn't limited to carne asada and guacamole! Switch it up with these waffle taco shells stuffed with ice cream. They're better than a sundae if you ask me, and maybe even better than a taco! 👁️👄👁️

SERVES 4

2 cups complete ("just add water") pancake mix

1½ cups water

3 tablespoons cocoa powder

3 tablespoons granulated sugar

⅛ teaspoon salt

8 (½-cup) scoops ice cream

3 tablespoons chocolate syrup

1 tablespoon rainbow sprinkles

1. Preheat mini-waffle maker to medium-high heat.

2. In a medium bowl, whisk together pancake mix, water, cocoa, sugar, and salt. Let batter rest 5 minutes.

3. Coat waffle maker with nonstick cooking spray and add ¼ of batter. Close waffle maker and cook 3 minutes.

4. Using tongs, remove waffle from waffle maker and shape into a taco by folding carefully. Set upright between two objects, like mugs, to cool. Repeat cooking and shaping with remaining batter.

5. Once all waffle tacos have cooled 5 minutes, place 2 scoops ice cream in each taco shell. Drizzle with syrup and add sprinkles on top. Eat immediately.

Cookie Mug Cake

Here's the easiest way to satisfy a sweet craving! This mug cake uses just two ingredients and tastes *sooo* good. It makes a superfluffy cake your audience will be drooling over.

SERVES 1

8 chocolate sandwich crème cookies
3 tablespoons whole milk

1. Add cookies to a large microwave-safe mug and pour milk on top.

2. Mash cookies with a fork to make a paste reminiscent of a cake batter.

3. Microwave on high 1½ minutes, then carefully remove from microwave and let cool 5 minutes.

4. Eat with a spoon.

#ForYou Tips

Something that works great with #foodTikTok? Series. In my case, I experimented with as many cookie options as possible, from sandwich crème cookies and chocolate chip to wafers and frosted sugar cookies. Whatever your top recipe video is, re-create it in different flavors to make your own series. This will get your followers excited and lead to great engagement. You can even ask them which version was their favorite and what to make next! 🎛️

Donut Bread Pudding

Everyone knows what to do when bread goes stale: make bread pudding! But what happens when leftover donuts go stale?! Well, let me tell you: You make Donut Bread Pudding.

SERVES 4

1 (7-ounce) can sweetened condensed milk

½ cup heavy cream

1 (14-ounce) can evaporated milk

2 medium eggs

1 teaspoon vanilla extract

¼ teaspoon kosher salt

½ teaspoon ground cinnamon

8 slightly hardened glazed donuts, cut into 1″ cubes

2 tablespoons powdered sugar

1. Preheat oven to 350°F. Coat an 8″ × 8″ baking pan with nonstick cooking spray.

2. In a large bowl, whisk together condensed milk, cream, evaporated milk, eggs, vanilla, salt, and cinnamon.

3. Place donut cubes in baking pan, forming an even layer.

4. Carefully pour milk mixture over donut cubes. Using the back of a spoon, lightly tap down on mixture to ensure an even layer and that mixture is evenly soaked throughout cubes. Cover with aluminum foil.

5. Bake 35 minutes. Remove foil and bake another 15 minutes.

6. Let cool 10 minutes and dust with sugar. Cut into fourths with a serrated knife and lift out onto large plates with a serving spatula.

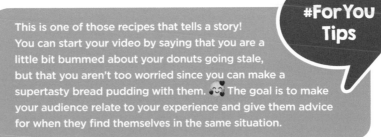

#For You Tips

This is one of those recipes that tells a story! You can start your video by saying that you are a little bit bummed about your donuts going stale, but that you aren't too worried since you can make a supertasty bread pudding with them. 😋 The goal is to make your audience relate to your experience and give them advice for when they find themselves in the same situation.

Fried Sandwich Cookies

The carnival classic we love! But guess what? You don't have to wait for the fair to come to town to enjoy these fried cookies: They're extremely easy to make at home.

MAKES 8 COOKIES

4 cups vegetable oil

1 cup complete ("just add water") pancake mix

¾ cup water

8 chocolate sandwich crème cookies

3 tablespoons powdered sugar

1. In a large pot over high heat, heat oil to 375°F. Line a medium bowl with paper towels.

2. In another medium bowl, whisk together pancake mix and water until there are no clumps left. Let batter rest 5 minutes.

3. Once oil is ready, coat each cookie individually in batter and carefully add to oil using tongs. Cook on each side 1 minute.

4. Remove cookies from oil with a spider strainer or tongs and place in prepared bowl.

5. Sprinkle cookies with sugar and serve.

1-Pound Air Fryer Cookie

TikTok is all about mini and supersized versions of food. I've taught you how to make cereal versions of muffins and pancakes; now it's time for a giant 1-pound cookie baked right in your air fryer!

SERVES 3

1 pound cookie dough
3 tablespoons hazelnut spread

1. Preheat air fryer to 270°F.

2. Divide dough in two pieces, forming one piece into a ball. Push down on center of ball to form a crater.

3. Add hazelnut spread to center of crater and place remaining dough on top. Press down lightly to seal and reshape into a ball.

4. Line air fryer basket with parchment paper and place cookie ball on center of paper. Bake 23 minutes or until golden.

5. Place on a wire rack to cool 15 minutes before eating.

#ForYou Tips

TikTok trends go hand in hand with holidays. Try using flavors based on the current season. Christmas time? Use Christmas tree cookie dough and add holiday sprinkles. Is it fall? Use snickerdoodle cookie dough and sprinkle pumpkin pie seasoning on top. Pair up the video with a fun holiday song, and your audience will love it! 🐼

Matcha Lava Cake

Nothing is more mesmerizing than a lava cake. It's indulgent, soft, and *sooo* delicious. The classic chocolate flavor is good, but this matcha version will for sure impress your followers. Nothing beats a pretty treat.

SERVES 2

⅓ cup white chocolate chips

3 tablespoons unsalted butter, melted

¼ cup granulated sugar

3 tablespoons sifted all-purpose flour

1 medium egg, beaten

2 teaspoons ceremonial matcha powder or 1 tablespoon food-grade matcha powder

1 tablespoon powdered sugar

1. Place chocolate chips in a large microwave-safe bowl and microwave on high 30 seconds. Stir and microwave another 20 seconds. Repeat cooking and stirring until fully melted.

2. Add butter and whisk together until incorporated. Add granulated sugar and whisk again. Slowly add in flour, then whisk.

3. Add egg, whisk again, then add matcha powder with a strainer. Whisk.

4. Coat two ramekins with nonstick cooking spray. Divide batter between ramekins, leaving 2″ of space at top. Place in freezer 45 minutes. When about 15 minutes remain, preheat oven to 400°F.

5. Place ramekins on center rack of oven and bake 15 minutes.

6. Remove from oven and use an oven mitt and tongs to flip over each ramekin onto a small plate. Using a sifter, dust powdered sugar on top. To eat, break in half using a spoon to release melted interior.

Unicorn Fudge

One of my favorite food trends has to be unicorn food! It calls up such a magical feeling—plus it's adorable. And fudge is one of those desserts that seems hard to make but is actually simple, especially when you use a microwave method instead of the classic stovetop. Use this recipe for fudge that is pure magic.

SERVES 8

1¼ cups white chocolate chips

1 (14-ounce) can sweetened condensed milk

1 teaspoon vanilla extract

1 tablespoon unsalted butter, melted

¼ teaspoon salt

6 drops each pink, blue, and purple food coloring

3 tablespoons rainbow sprinkles

1. Add chocolate chips to a large microwave-safe bowl and microwave on high 30 seconds. Stir and microwave another 30 seconds. Repeat cooking and stirring until fully melted.

2. Add condensed milk, vanilla, butter, and salt to bowl and stir until fully combined. Separate mixture into three small bowls.

3. Add 6 drops food coloring to each bowl and stir, using different spoons so colors don't mix. Line an 8″ × 8″ baking pan with plastic wrap or aluminum foil.

4. Drop 2 tablespoons of each colored batter into pan at a time until all batter is used up. Swirl top using a toothpick or knife. Scatter sprinkles on top.

5. Refrigerate covered in plastic wrap at least 4 hours. Once solid, remove from pan and gently peel off plastic wrap/foil. Using a knife, cut into 1″ squares. Fudge will keep covered in fridge up to 3 days.

Grilled S'more

Grilled cheese used to be my ultimate childhood snack. But part of growing up is realizing that you no longer have to follow any rules and that you can make a dessert out of anything. So I present to you my new fave, the Grilled S'more!

SERVES 1

1 tablespoon unsalted butter

2 slices white bread

2 tablespoons marshmallow crème

1 (2-ounce) bar milk chocolate, sliced into long, thin pieces

1. On a large griddle over medium heat, melt butter, then add bread.

2. Spread marshmallow crème over 1 slice. Place chocolate pieces on top of marshmallow. Allow bread to toast and marshmallow and chocolate to melt, about 3 minutes.

3. Place second slice on top to make a sandwich and move to a cutting board. Cut diagonally and serve on a medium plate.

3-Minute Donuts

Donuts can seem hard to make, but all you need for this version is canned biscuits, an air fryer, and some basic ingredients you probably already have! It may be the easiest dessert recipe ever. These are the ✦ new ✦ apple cider donuts.

MAKES 8 DONUTS

1 (16-ounce) can large butter biscuits

½ cup powdered sugar

2 tablespoons cocoa powder

1½ tablespoons whole milk

3 tablespoons rainbow sprinkles

1. Preheat air fryer to 370°F.

2. Separate biscuits and lay flat on a cutting board. Using a cookie cutter or knife, make a 1″ hole in center of each. Discard centers or use to make donut holes.

3. Place donuts in ungreased air fryer basket, being careful not to crowd them, and cook 3 minutes.

4. While donuts cook, whisk together sugar, cocoa, and milk in a medium bowl.

5. Once donuts are ready, place them on a wire rack to cool 2 minutes. When cool enough to handle, dip donuts in icing and top with sprinkles. Allow icing to harden 25 minutes before eating.

Marshmallow Popcorn Balls

I think everyone is tired of seeing and eating marshmallow cereal bars. Sure, they're delicious, but so outdated! So let's spice things up and use up the microwave popcorn sitting in your pantry for something a little more interesting.

SERVES 10

20 large marshmallows
2 tablespoons unsalted butter
2 cups plain popped popcorn

1. In a large microwave-safe bowl, combine marshmallows and butter. Microwave on high 45 seconds, then stir. Repeat cooking and stirring until fully melted.

2. Add popcorn to bowl and stir until fully coated in marshmallow mixture.

3. Line a large baking sheet with parchment paper. Spray your hands with nonstick cooking spray to stop popcorn from sticking to your fingers.

4. Take ⅓ cup popcorn mixture at a time and form into a ball. Place on prepared baking sheet. Repeat with remaining popcorn mixture. Let balls cool 10 minutes before eating.

Mini Baked Donuts

I can't stress it enough: Everything is cuter when it's miniature. These baked donuts are supereasy to make, healthier than regular donuts, and so, so fluffy. They're what the Japanese call *#kawaii* ("cute")!

MAKES 24 MINI DONUTS

1 cup all-purpose flour

⅓ cup granulated sugar

1 tablespoon baking powder

½ teaspoon salt

1 medium egg

2 tablespoons unsalted butter, melted

½ cup whole milk

1 tablespoon vanilla extract

½ cup powdered sugar

2 tablespoons water

6 drops food coloring

3 tablespoons rainbow sprinkles

1. Preheat oven to 350°F. Spray a twelve-cavity mini-donut mold with nonstick cooking spray.

2. In a large bowl, whisk together flour, sugar, baking powder, and salt. Add egg, butter, milk, and vanilla and whisk again to combine.

3. Add batter to a piping bag or plastic bag. Cut a ½" hole in bag and pipe into mold.

4. Bake 8 minutes.

5. While donuts bake, mix together sugar, water, and food coloring in a small bowl.

6. Remove donuts from oven, let cool 2 minutes, then dip in glaze to cover top of each donut. Place on a wire rack and top with rainbow sprinkles.

7. Allow icing to set 15 minutes before eating.

S'mores Cookie Cups

Marshmallows are the perfect dessert add-on. They taste amazing, but they also add that stretchy element that drives people wild. These cookie cups take only a couple of minutes to make and will get your audience hyped!

SERVES 12

2¼ cups chocolate chip cookie dough
12 large marshmallows
1 (4.4-ounce) milk chocolate bar, divided into 12 pieces

1. Preheat oven to 350°F. Spray a twelve-cup muffin tin with nonstick cooking spray.

2. Add 3 tablespoons dough to each cup and press down using your fingers to cover bottom and sides of cups. Place 1 marshmallow in each cup.

3. Bake 14 minutes.

4. Remove tin from oven and preheat broiler to high. Broil 2 minutes or until marshmallows are just browned.

5. Remove tin from oven and immediately top cups with chocolate pieces.

6. Allow to cool in pan 10 minutes, then remove using a spoon. Serve on a large plate.

#ForYou Tips

We all know what a cheese pull is, but what about a marshmallow pull? These are just as mesmerizing! It's one of the best and most interactive ways of showing off a dessert. Make a video of yourself baking this recipe (be sure to let the cups cool off before taking them out of the tin). For the final shot, to get the melted marshmallow effect, reheat the cups by popping them in the microwave 30 seconds. With both your hands, slowly break a cup apart on camera and spread out the pieces to create a long thread of melty marshmallow. Highlighting the #foodporn qualities of your masterpiece is how you get the likes.

Stuffed Cookie Skillet

Cookie skillets are a classic at restaurants and *sooo* delicious! They might seem like they'd be supercomplicated to make at home, but all you really need is a small cast iron skillet, cookie dough...and maybe some self-control because you'll want to eat it all yourself.

SERVES 4

1 (30-ounce) package chocolate chip cookie dough, divided in half

¼ cup hazelnut spread

⅛ teaspoon flaky salt

1 (½-cup) scoop vanilla ice cream

1. Preheat oven to 350°F. Grease a small cast iron skillet with nonstick cooking spray.

2. Place half of dough in prepared skillet. Press down with your fingers to cover bottom of skillet and 1″ up sides.

3. Using a spatula, add hazelnut spread to center of dough and spread to create a circle 3½″ in diameter.

4. Over a flat surface, press down remaining dough to form a disk the same size as skillet. With both hands, lift up dough disk and place directly on top of hazelnut spread. Press down along edges to close.

5. Sprinkle salt on top and bake 15 minutes.

6. Remove from oven and cool 5 minutes. Add ice cream on top and eat directly out of skillet with spoons, or transfer to four small plates.

Edible Cookie Dough

Did Mom ever tell you to stop eating raw cookie dough or you'd get sick? Well, now you can eat all the dough you want! It's better to be safe than sorry—plus, this tastes like the real deal! ✨

SERVES 5

2 cups all-purpose flour

1 cup unsalted butter, softened

1 cup light brown sugar

1 teaspoon vanilla extract

½ teaspoon sea salt

3 tablespoons whole milk

¼ cup mini milk chocolate chips

¼ cup rainbow sprinkles

1. Add flour to a large microwave-safe bowl and microwave on high 60 seconds. Stir and microwave another 60 seconds. Repeat stirring and cooking one more time until flour reaches 165°F.

2. Add all remaining ingredients except chocolate chips and sprinkles to bowl. Stir until fully combined. Cover and refrigerate 30 minutes.

3. When dough is chilled, divide into two medium bowls and add chocolate chips to one bowl and sprinkles to the other. Dough will keep covered in fridge up to 5 days.

Kitchen Hacks

Edible cookie dough is superpopular on social media—maybe because of the memories it brings back of cookies baking in the oven when you were a kid. Cookie dough is also so versatile that it can be added as a topping to anything! Use it to top brownies, ice cream sundaes, cakes—whatever calls to you. You can roll it into little balls for cookie dough bites or serve it in a waffle cone and eat it like ice cream.

Standard US/Metric Measurement Conversions

VOLUME CONVERSIONS

US Volume Measure	Metric Equivalent
⅛ teaspoon	0.5 milliliter
¼ teaspoon	1 milliliter
½ teaspoon	2 milliliters
1 teaspoon	5 milliliters
½ tablespoon	7 milliliters
1 tablespoon (3 teaspoons)	15 milliliters
2 tablespoons (1 fluid ounce)	30 milliliters
¼ cup (4 tablespoons)	60 milliliters
⅓ cup	90 milliliters
½ cup (4 fluid ounces)	125 milliliters
⅔ cup	160 milliliters
¾ cup (6 fluid ounces)	180 milliliters
1 cup (16 tablespoons)	250 milliliters
1 pint (2 cups)	500 milliliters
1 quart (4 cups)	1 liter (about)

WEIGHT CONVERSIONS

US Weight Measure	Metric Equivalent
½ ounce	15 grams
1 ounce	30 grams
2 ounces	60 grams
3 ounces	85 grams
¼ pound (4 ounces)	115 grams
½ pound (8 ounces)	225 grams
¾ pound (12 ounces)	340 grams
1 pound (16 ounces)	454 grams

OVEN TEMPERATURE CONVERSIONS

Degrees Fahrenheit	Degrees Celsius
200 degrees F	95 degrees C
250 degrees F	120 degrees C
275 degrees F	135 degrees C
300 degrees F	150 degrees C
325 degrees F	160 degrees C
350 degrees F	180 degrees C
375 degrees F	190 degrees C
400 degrees F	205 degrees C
425 degrees F	220 degrees C
450 degrees F	230 degrees C

BAKING PAN SIZES

American	Metric
8 × 1½ inch round baking pan	20 × 4 cm cake tin
9 × 1½ inch round baking pan	23 × 3.5 cm cake tin
11 × 7 × 1½ inch baking pan	28 × 18 × 4 cm baking tin
13 × 9 × 2 inch baking pan	30 × 20 × 5 cm baking tin
2 quart rectangular baking dish	30 × 20 × 3 cm baking tin
15 × 10 × 2 inch baking pan	30 × 25 × 2 cm baking tin (Swiss roll tin)
9 inch pie plate	22 × 4 or 23 × 4 cm pie plate
7 or 8 inch springform pan	18 or 20 cm springform or loose bottom cake tin
9 × 5 × 3 inch loaf pan	23 × 13 × 7 cm or 2 lb narrow loaf or pate tin
1½ quart casserole	1.5 liter casserole
2 quart casserole	2 liter casserole

Index

NOTES

NOTES

NOTES

NOTES

Valentina Mussi is a food and lifestyle content creator based in Miami. She comes from an Italian-Colombian family, and her culturally diverse background has given her a unique outlook on food and culture. Her sweet tooth and love for good food drove her to start Sweetportfolio, a verified account and social media brand where she showcases fun and easy recipes. Among her most popular videos are her Crusted Round Cheese recipe coming in at more than 29 million total views, her Whipped Strawberry Milk at more than 26 million total views, and her Mermaid Milkshake at more than 19 million total views. Her easy-to-follow and simple—yet eye-catching—recipes have captured the attention of not only social media users but major media outlets as well, including *Time, Insider, People,* ABC News, and *Today*.